Born and raised in Hawaii, **Robert T. Kiyosaki** co-founded an international education company that operated in seven countries, teaching business to tens of thousands of graduates. Now retired, Robert does what he enjoys most . . . he invests. Concerned about the growing gap between the haves and have nots, Robert created the board game Cashflow, which teaches the game of money, before only known by the rich.

Sharon L. Lechter is a wife, the mother of three, a consultant to the toy and publishing industries, and a business owner. As co-author of the *Rich Dad, Poor Dad* books, she now focuses her efforts in helping to create educational tools for anyone interested in bettering their own financial education.

Also by Robert T. Kiyosaki with Sharon L. Lechter

RICH DAD, POOR DAD
RICH DAD'S GUIDE TO INVESTING
RICH DAD'S RICH KID, SMART KID
RICH DAD'S RETIRE YOUNG, RETIRE RICH
RICH DAD'S PROPHECY

RICH DAD, POOR DAD 2:
Cashflow Quadrant

**Employee, Self-employed,
Business Owner, or Investor . . .
Which is the best Quadrant for you?**

BY ROBERT T. KIYOSAKI
WITH SHARON L. LECHTER C.P.A.

timewarner
paperbacks

A *Time Warner* Paperback

First published in the United States in 2000 by Warner Books, Inc.,
in association with CASHFLOW Technologies, Inc.

First published in Great Britain in 2002 by Time Warner Paperbacks
Reprinted 2003, 2004

Copyright © 1998, 1999 by Robert T. Kiyosaki
and Sharon L. Lechter

'CASHFLOW' is the trademark of Cashflow Technologies, Inc.

are trademarks of CASHFLOW Technologies, Inc.

The moral right of the authors has been asserted.

A CIP catalogue record for this book
is available from the British Library.

ISBN 0 7515 3280 0

Typeset by Palimpsest Book Production Limited,
Polmont, Stirlingshire
Printed and bound in Great Britain by
Clays Ltd, St Ives plc

Time Warner Paperbacks
An imprint of
Time Warner Book Group UK
Brettenham House
Lancaster Place
London WC2E 7EN

www.twbg.co.uk

'Man is born free;
and everywhere he is in chains.
One thinks himself the master of others,
and still remains a greater slave than they.'

Jean Jacques Rousseau

My rich dad used to say, 'You can never have
true freedom without financial freedom.' He
would go on to say, 'Freedom may be free, but
it has a price.' This book is dedicated to those
people willing to pay the price.

To Our Friends,

The phenomenal success of *Rich Dad Poor Dad* has brought us thousands of new friends all over the world. Their kind words and friendship inspired us to write *The CASHFLOW Quadrant* which, in reality, is a continuation of *Rich Dad Poor Dad*.

So to our friends, old and new, for their enthusiastic support beyond our wildest dreams, we say thank you.

Table of Contents

**THE 7 STEPS TO FINDING
YOUR FINANCIAL FAST TRACK**

Which Quadrant Are You In? Is It The Right One For You?

Are you financially free? *The CASHFLOW Quadrant* was written for you if your life has come to a financial fork in the road. If you want to take control of what you do today in order to change your financial destiny it will help you chart your course. This is the *CASHFLOW Quadrant*:

The letters in each quadrant represent:

E for employee

S for self-employed

B for business owner

I for investor

Each of us resides in at least one of the four quadrants of the *CASHFLOW Quadrant*. Where we are is determined by where our cash comes from. Many of us rely on paychecks and are therefore employees, while others are self-employed. Employees and self-employed individuals reside on the left side of the *CASHFLOW Quadrant*. The right side of the *CASHFLOW Quadrant* is for individuals who receive their cash from businesses they own or investments they own.

The CASHFLOW Quadrant is about the four different types of people who make up the world of business, who they are and what makes individuals in each quadrant unique. It will help you define where you are in the *Quadrant* today and help you chart a course for where you want to be in the future as you choose your own path to financial freedom. While financial freedom can be found in all four of the quadrants, the skills of a 'B' or 'I' will help you reach your financial goals more quickly. A successful 'E' should also become a successful 'I'.

What Do You Want To Be When You Grow Up?

This book is in many ways Part II of my book, *Rich Dad Poor Dad*. For those of you who may not have read *Rich Dad Poor Dad*, it was about the different lessons my two dads taught me about the subject of money and life choices. One was my real dad and the other my best friend's dad. One was highly educated and the other a high school drop out. One was poor and the other rich.

Whenever I was asked the question, 'What do you want to be when you grow up?'

My highly educated but poor dad always recommended,

'Go to school, get good grades, and then find a safe secure job.'

He was recommending a life's path that looked like this.

Poor Dad's Advice

Poor dad was recommending that I choose to become either a high paid 'E', employee, or a high paid 'S', self-employed professional, such as a medical doctor, lawyer, or accountant. My poor dad was very concerned about a steady paycheck, benefits, and job security. That is why he was a high paid government official; the head of education for the State of Hawaii.

My rich, but uneducated dad, on the other hand, offered very different advice. He recommended,

'Go to school, graduate, build businesses and become a successful investor.'

He was recommending a life's path that looked like this.

Rich Dad's Advice

This book is about the mental, emotional, and educational process I went through in following my rich dad's advice.

Who This Book Is For

This book is written for people who are ready to change quadrants. This book is especially for individuals who are currently in the 'E' and 'S' categories and are contemplating becoming 'B's' or 'I's'. It is for people who are ready to move beyond job security and begin to achieve financial security. It is not an easy life's path but the prize at the end of the journey is worth the journey. It is the journey to financial freedom.

Rich dad told me a simple story when I was 12 years old that has guided me to great wealth and financial freedom. It was rich dad's way of explaining the difference between the left side of the *CASHFLOW Quadrant*, the 'E' and 'S' quadrants, from the right side or the 'B' and 'I' quadrants. It goes:

'Once upon a time there was this quaint little village. It was a great place to live except for one problem. The village had no water unless it rained. To solve this problem once and for all, the village elders decided to put out to bid the contract to have water delivered to the village on a daily basis. Two people volunteered to take on the task and the olders awarded the contract to both of them. They felt that a little competition would keep prices low and insure a back up supply of water.

The first of the two people who won the contract, Ed, immediately ran out, bought two galvanized steel buckets and began running back and forth along the trail to the lake which was a mile away. He immediately began making money as he labored morning to dusk hauling water from the lake with his two buckets. He would empty them into the large concrete holding tank the village had built. Each morning he had to get up before the rest of the village awoke to make sure there was enough water for the village when it wanted it. It was hard work, but he was very happy

4

to be making money and for having one of the two exclusive contracts for this business.

The second winning contractor, Bill, disappeared for a while. He was not seen for months, which made Ed very happy since he had no competition. Ed was making all the money.

Instead of buying two buckets to compete with Ed, Bill had written a business plan, created a corporation, found four investors, employed a president to do the work, and returned six months later with a construction crew. Within a year his team had built a large volume stainless steel pipeline which connected the village to the lake.

At the grand opening celebration, Bill announced that his water was cleaner than Ed's water. Bill knew that there had been complaints about dirt in Ed's water. Bill also announced that he could supply the village with water 24 hours a day, 7 days a week. Ed could only deliver water on the weekdays . . . he did not work on weekends. Then Bill announced that he would charge 75% less than Ed did for this higher quality and more reliable source of water. The village cheered and ran immediately for the faucet at the end of Bill's pipeline.

In order to compete, Ed immediately lowered his rates by 75%, bought two more buckets, added covers to his buckets and began hauling four buckets each trip. In order to provide better service, he hired his two sons to give him a hand for the night shift and on weekends. When his boys went off to college, he said to them, "Hurry back because someday this business will belong to you."

For some reason, after college, his two sons never returned. Eventually Ed had employee and union problems. The union was demanding higher wages, better benefits, and wanted its members to only haul one bucket at a time.

Bill, on the other hand, realized that if this village needed water then other villages must need water too. He rewrote his business plan and went off to sell his high speed, high volume, low cost, and clean water delivery system to villages throughout the world. He only makes a penny per bucket of water delivered, but he delivers billions of buckets of water everyday. Regardless if he works or not, billions of people consume billions of buckets of water, and all that money pours into his bank account. Bill had developed a pipeline to deliver money to himself as well as water to the villages.

Bill lived happily ever after and Ed worked hard for the rest of his life and had financial problems forever after. The end.'

That story about Bill and Ed has guided me for years. It has assisted me in my life's decision making process. I often ask myself,

'Am I building a pipeline or hauling buckets?'

'Am I working hard or am I working smart?'

And the answers to those questions have made me financially free.

And that is what this book is about. It is about what it takes to become a 'B' and an 'I'. It is for people who are tired of hauling buckets and are ready to build pipelines for cash to flow into their pockets . . . not out of their pockets.

This Book Is Divided Into Three Parts

Part One: The first part of this book is about the core differences between people in the four quadrants. It is about why certain people gravitate to certain quadrants and often get stuck there without realizing it. It will help you identify where you are today in the *Quadrant* and where you want to be in five years.

Part Two: The second part of this book is about personal change. It is more about 'who' you have to be instead of what you have to do.

Part Three: The third part of this book defines seven steps you can take on your path to the right side of the *Quadrant*. I will share more of my rich dad's secrets on the skills required to be a successful 'B' and 'I'. It will help you choose your own path to financial freedom.

6

Throughout *The CASHFLOW Quadrant* I continue to stress the importance of financial intelligence. If you want to operate on the right side of the quadrant, the 'B' and 'I' side, a person needs to be smarter than if you choose to stay on the left side as an 'E' or 'S'.

To be a 'B' or 'I', you must be able to control the direction your cash flow is flowing. This book is written for people who are ready to make changes in their lives. It is written for people who are ready to move beyond job security and begin to build their own pipelines to achieve financial freedom.

We are in the dawning of the Information Age and this age will offer more opportunities than ever before for financial reward. It will be individuals with the skills of the 'B's' and 'I's' who will be able to identify and seize those opportunities. To be successful in the Information Age, a person will need information from all four quadrants. Unfortunately, our schools are still in the Industrial Age and still prepare students for only the left side of the *Quadrant*.

If you are looking for new answers to move forward into the Information Age, then this book is written for you. It is written to assist you in your journey into the Information Age. It does not have all the answers . . . but it will share the deep personal and guiding insights I gained as I traveled from the 'E' and 'S' side of the *CASHFLOW Quadrant*, to the 'B' and 'I' side.

If you are ready to begin your journey or are already on your journey to financial freedom this book is written for you.

As my way of saying 'Thank You' for reading this book and increasing your knowledge about money and business, I make available to you a special audio report entitled,

'What My Rich Dad Taught Me About Investing.'

It is an educational tape that offers further insights into what my rich dad taught me about investing. It is offered to further enhance your education and explain why we create our educational products for people like you. With a retail value of $19.95 we offer this tape as a gift to you.

This tape does not discuss what I call 'Middle Class' investment strategies . . . especially those heavily dependent upon mutual funds. In fact you will find out why many rich people don't buy mutual funds. As with all our products, we do our best to provide distinctions between how the rich, the poor, and the middle class think . . . and then leave the choice up to you as to which way you want to think. After all, one of the benefits of living in a free society is that we all have the choice to be rich, poor, or middle class. That decision is up to you, regardless of which class you are in today.

All you have to do to get this audio report is visit our special website at www.richdadbook2.com and the report is yours free.

Thank you

PART ONE

THE CASHFLOW QUADRANT

CHAPTER ONE

'Why Don't You Get A Job?'

In 1985, my wife, Kim, and I were homeless. We were unemployed and had little money left from our savings; our credit cards were exhausted; and we lived in an old brown Toyota with reclining seats that served as beds. At the end of one week, the harsh reality of who we were, what we were doing, and where we were headed began to sink in.

Our homelessness lasted for another two weeks. A friend, when she realized our desperate financial situation, offered us a room in her basement. We lived there for nine months.

We kept our situation quiet. For the most part, my wife and I looked quite normal on the surface. When friends and family were informed of our plight, the first question was always, 'Why don't you get a job?'

At first we attempted to explain, but in most instances, we failed to clarify our reasons. To someone who values a job, it is difficult to explain why you might not want a job.

Occasionally, we did a few odd jobs and earned a few dollars here and there. But we did that only to keep food in our stomachs and gas in the car. Those few extra dollars were only fuel to keep us going toward our singular goal. I must admit that during moments of deep personal doubt, the idea of a safe, secure job with a paycheck was appealing. But because job security was not what we were looking for, we kept pushing on, living day to day, on the brink of the financial abyss.

That year, 1985, was the worst of our lives, as well as one of the longest. Anyone who says that money isn't important obviously has not been without it for long. Kim and I fought and argued often. Fear, uncertainty and hunger shortens the human emotional fuse, and often we fight with the person who loves us the most. Yet, love held the two of us together and our bond as a couple grew stronger because of the adversity. We knew where we were going; we just did not know if we would ever get there.

We knew we could always find a safe, secure, high-paying job. Both of us were college graduates with good job skills and solid work ethics. But we were not going for job security. We were going for financial freedom.

By 1989, we were millionaires. Although financially successful in some people's eyes, we still had not reached our dreams. We had not yet achieved true financial freedom. That took until 1994. By then, we never had to work again for the rest of our lives. Barring any unforeseen financial disaster, we were both financially free. Kim was 37, and I was 47.

It Doesn't Take Money To Make Money

I started this book about being homeless and having nothing because I often hear people say, 'It takes money to make money.'

I disagree. To get from homeless in 1985 to rich in 1989 and then to become financially free by 1994 did not take money. We had no money when we started, and we were in debt.

It also does not take a good formal education. I have a college degree, and I can honestly say that achieving financial freedom had nothing to do with what I learned in college. I did not find much call for my years of studying calculus, spherical trigonometry, chemistry, physics, French, and English literature.

Many successful people have left school without receiving a college degree. People such as Thomas Edison, founder of General Electric; Henry Ford, founder of Ford Motor Co.; Bill Gates, founder of Microsoft; Ted Turner, founder of CNN; Michael Dell, founder of Dell Computers; Steve Jobs, founder of Apple Computer; and Ralph Lauren, founder of Polo. A college education is important for traditional professions, but not for how these people found great wealth. They developed their own successful business and that was what Kim and I were striving for.

So What Does It Take?

I am often asked, 'If it doesn't take money to make money, and schools do not teach you how to become financially free, then what does it take?'

My answer: It takes a dream, a lot of determination, a willingness to learn quickly, and the ability to use your God-given assets properly and to know which sector of the *CASHFLOW Quadrant* to generate your income from.

What Is The Cashflow Quadrant?

The diagram below is the *CASHFLOW Quadrant*.

The letters in each quadrant represent:
E for employee
S for self-employed
B for business owner
I for investor

Which Quadrant Do You Generate Your Income From?

The *CASHFLOW Quadrant* represents the different methods by which income or money is generated. For example, an employee earns money by holding a job and working for someone else or a company. Self-employed people earn money working for themselves. A business owner owns a business that generates money, and investors earn money from their various investments – in other words, money generating more money.

Different methods of income generation require different frames of mind, different technical skills, different educational paths, and different types of people. Different people are attracted to different quadrants.

While money is all the same, the way it is earned can be vastly different. If you begin to look at the four different labels for each quadrant, you might want to ask yourself, 'Which quadrant do you generate the majority of your income from?'

Each quadrant is different. To generate income from different quadrants requires different skills and a different personality, even if the person found in each quadrant is the same. Changing from quadrant to quadrant is like playing golf in the morning and then attending the ballet at night.

You Can Earn Income In All Four Quadrants

Most of us have the potential to generate income from all four quadrants. Which quadrant you or I choose to earn our primary income from is not so much what we learned in school; it is more about who we are at the core – our core values, strengths, weaknesses and interests. It is these core differences that attract us to or repel us from the four quadrants.

Yet, regardless of what we 'do' professionally, we can still work in all four quadrants. For example, a medical doctor could choose to earn income as an 'E,' an employee, and join the staff of a large hospital, or work for the government in the public-health service, or become a military doctor, or join the staff of an insurance company needing a doctor on its staff.

This same doctor could also decide to earn income as an 'S,' a self-employed person, and start a private practice, setting up an office, hiring staff and building a private list of clients.

Or the doctor could decide to become a 'B' and own a clinic or laboratory and have other doctors on staff. This doctor probably would hire a business manager to run the organization. In this case, the doctor would own the business, but not have to work in it. The doctor also could decide to own a business that has nothing to do with the medical field, while still practicing medicine some-where else. In this case, the doctor would be earning income as both an 'E' and as a 'B.'

As an 'I,' the doctor also could generate income from being an investor in someone else's business or in vehicles like the stock market, bond market and real estate.

The important words are 'generate income from.' It is not so much what we do, but more how we generate income.

Different Methods of Income Generation

More than anything, it is the internal differences of our core values, strengths, weaknesses and interests that affect which quadrant we decide to generate our income from. Some people love being employees, while others hate it. Some people love owning compa-nies, but do not want to run them. Others love owning companies and also love running them. Certain people love investing, while others only see the risk of losing money. Most of us are a little of each of these characters. Being successful in the four quadrants often means redirecting some internal core values.

You Can Be Rich Or Poor In All Four Quadrants

It also is important to note that you can be rich or poor in all four quadrants. There are people who earn millions and people who go bankrupt in each of the quadrants. Being in one quadrant or the other does not necessarily guarantee financial success.

Not All Quadrants Are Equal

By knowing the different features of each quadrant, you'll have a better idea as to which quadrant, or quadrants, might be best for you.

For example, one of the many reasons I chose to work predominantly in the 'B' and 'I' quadrants is because of tax advantages. For most people working on the left side of the *Quadrant*, there are few legal tax breaks available. Yet, legal tax breaks abound on the right side of the *Quadrant*. By working to generate income in the 'B' and 'I' quadrants, I could acquire money faster and keep that money working for me longer, without losing large chunks to pay taxes.

Different Ways Of Earning Money

When people ask why Kim and I were homeless, I tell them it was because of what my rich dad taught me about money. For me, money is important, yet I did not want to spend my life working for it. That is why I did not want a job. If we were going to be responsible citizens, Kim and I wanted to have our money work for us rather than spend our lives physically working for money.

That is why the *CASHFLOW Quadrant* is important. It distinguishes between the different ways in which money is generated. There are ways of being responsible and creating money, other than physically working for it.

Different Fathers – Different Ideas About Money

My highly educated dad had a strong belief that the love of money was evil. That to profit excessively meant you were greedy. He felt embarrassed when the newspapers published how much he made, because he felt he was too highly paid when compared with the schoolteachers who worked for him. He was a good, honest, hard-working man who did his best to defend his point of view that money was not important to his life.

My highly educated, yet poor, dad constantly said,
'I'm not that interested in money.'
'I'll never be rich.'
'I can't afford it.'
'Investing is risky.'
'Money isn't everything.'

Money Supports Life

My rich dad had a different point of view. He thought it foolish to spend your life working for money and to pretend that money was not important. Rich dad believed that life was more important than money, but money was important for supporting life. He often said, 'You only have so many hours in a day and you can only work so hard. So why work hard for money? Learn to have money and people work hard for you, and you can be free to do the things that are important.'

To my rich dad, what was important was:
1. Having lots of time to raise his kids.
2. Having money to donate to charities and projects he supported.
3. Bringing jobs and financial stability to the community.
4. Having time and money to take care of his health.
5. Being able to travel the world with his family.

'Those things take money,' said rich dad. 'That is why money is important to me. Money is important, but I don't want to spend my life working for it.'

Choosing The Quadrants

One reason my wife and I focused on the 'B' and 'I' quadrants while we were homeless was because I had more training and education in those quadrants. It was because of my rich dad's guidance that I knew the different financial and professional advantages of each quadrant. For me, the quadrants of the right side, the 'B' and 'I' quadrants, offered the best opportunity for financial success and financial freedom.

Also, at 37 years old, I had experienced successes and failures in all four quadrants, which allowed me some degree of understanding about my own personal temperament, likes, dislikes, strengths and weaknesses. I knew which quadrants I did best in.

Parents Are Teachers

It was my rich dad who often referred to the *CASHFLOW Quadrant* when I was a young boy. He would explain to me the difference between someone who was successful on the left side vs. the right side. Yet being young, I really did not pay much attention to what he said. I did not understand the difference between an employee's mind-set and a business owner's mind-set. I was just trying to survive in school.

Yet, I did hear his words, and soon his words began to make sense. Having two dynamic and successful father figures around me gave meaning to what each was saying. But it was what they were doing that allowed me to begin to notice the differences between the 'E–S' side of the *Quadrant* and the 'B–I' side. At first the differences were subtle, and then they became glaring.

For example, one painful lesson I experienced as a young boy was simply how much time one dad had available to spend with me vs. the other. As the success and prominence of both dads grew, it was obvious that one dad had less and less time to spend with his wife and four children. My real dad was always on the road, at meetings, or dashing off to the airport for more meetings.

The more successful he got, the fewer dinners we had together as a family. Weekends, he spent at home in his crowded little office, buried under paperwork.

My rich dad, on the other hand, had more and more free time as his success grew. One of the reasons I learned so much about money, finance, business and life was simply because my rich dad had more and more free time for his children and me.

Another example is that both dads made more and more money as they became successful, but my real dad, the educated one, also got further into debt. So he'd work harder and suddenly find himself in a higher income-tax bracket. His banker and accountant would then tell him to buy a bigger house for the so-called 'tax break.' My dad would follow the advice and buy a bigger house, and soon he was working harder than ever so he could make more money to pay for the new house . . . taking him even further away from his family.

My rich dad was different. He made more and more money, but paid less in taxes. He, too, had bankers and accountants, but he was not getting the same advice my highly educated dad was getting.

The Main Reason

Yet, the driving force that would not allow me to stay on the left side of the *Quadrant* was what happened to my highly educated but poor dad at the peak of his career.

In the early 1970s, I was already out of college and in Pensacola, Florida, going through pilot training for the Marine Corps, on my way to Vietnam. My educated dad was now the Superintendent of Education for the State of Hawaii and a member of the governor's staff. One evening, my dad phoned me in my room on base.

'Son,' he said. 'I'm going to resign from my job and run for lieutenant governor of the state of Hawaii for the Republican Party.'

I gulped and then said, 'You're going to run for office against your boss?'

'That's right,' he replied.

'Why?' I asked. 'Republicans do not have a chance in Hawaii. The Democratic Party and the labor unions are too strong.'

'I know, son. I also know that we do not have a prayer of winning. Judge Samuel King will be the candidate for governor, and I will be his running mate.'

'Why?' I asked again. 'Why run against your boss if you know you're going to lose?'

'Because my conscience won't let me do anything else. The games these politicians are playing disturb me.'

'Are you saying they're corrupt?' I asked.

'I don't want to say that,' said my real dad. He was an honest and moral man who rarely spoke badly about anyone. He was always a diplomat. Yet, I could tell from his voice that he was angry and upset when he said, 'I'll just say that my conscience bothers me when I see what goes on behind the scenes. I could not live with myself if I turned a blind eye and did nothing. My job and paycheck are not as important as my conscience.'

After a long silence, I realized that my dad's mind was made up. 'Good luck,' I said quietly. 'I'm proud of you for your courage, and I'm proud to be your son.'

My dad and the Republican ticket were crushed, as expected. The re-elected governor sent the word out that my dad was never to get a job again with the government for the state of Hawaii . . . and he never did. At the age of 54, my dad went looking for a job, and I was on my way to Vietnam.

At middle age my dad was looking for a new job. He went from jobs with big titles and low pay to more jobs with big titles and low pay. Jobs where he was the executive director of XYZ Services, a nonprofit organization, or managing director of ABC Services, another nonprofit.

He was a tall, brilliant and dynamic man who was no longer welcome in the only world he knew, the world of government employees. He tried starting several small businesses. He was a consultant for a while, and even bought a famous franchise, but they all failed. As he grew older, and his strength slipped away, so did his drive to start over again; his lack of will became even more pronounced after each business failure. He was a successful 'E' trying to survive as an 'S,' a quadrant in which he had no training or experience and for which he had no heart. He loved the world of public education, but he could not find a way to get back in. The ban on his employment in the state government was silently in place. In some circles, the word is called 'blacklisted.'

If not for Social Security and Medicare, the last years of his life would have been a complete disaster. He died frustrated and a little angry, yet he died with a clear conscience.

So what kept me going in the darkest of hours? It was the haunting memory of my educated dad sitting at home, waiting for the phone to ring, trying to succeed in the world of business, a world he knew nothing about.

That, and the joyous memory of seeing my rich dad grow happier and more successful as his years went on inspired me. Instead of declining at age 54, rich dad blossomed. He had become rich years before that, but now he was becoming mega-rich. He was constantly in the newspapers as the man who was buying up Waikiki and Maui. His years of methodically building businesses and investing was paying off, and he was on his way to becoming one of the richest men in the Islands.

Small Differences Become Large Differences

Because my rich dad had explained the *Quadrant* to me, I was better able to see the small differences that grew into large differences when measured over the years a person spends working. Because of the *Quadrant*, I knew it was better to decide not so much what I wanted to do, but more who I wanted to become as my working years progressed. In the darkest hours, it was this deep knowledge, and lessons from two powerful dads, that kept me going.

It Is More Than The Quadrant

The *CASHFLOW Quadrant* is more than two lines and some letters.

If you look below the surface of this simple diagram, you will find completely different worlds as well as different ways of looking at the world. As a person who has looked at the world from both the left side of the *Quadrant* and the right side, I can honestly say the world looks much different depending on which side you are on . . . and those differences are what this book is about.

One quadrant is not better than another . . . each has strengths, and each has weaknesses. This book is written to allow you to glimpse into the different quadrants, and into the personal development required to be financially successful in each of them. It is my hope that you will gain further insights into choosing the financial life path that is best suited for you.

Many of the skills essential to be successful on the right side of the *Quadrant* are not taught in school, which might explain why people like Bill Gates of Microsoft, and Ted Turner of CNN, and Thomas Edison left school early. This book will identify the skills, as well as the personal core temperament, that are necessary to find success on the 'B' and 'I' side of the *Quadrant*.

First, I offer a broad overview of the four quadrants and then a closer focus on the 'B' and 'I' side. There are already plenty of books written about what it takes to be successful on the 'E' and 'S' side.

After reading this book, some of you might want to make a change in how you earn your income, and some of you will be happy to stay just where you are. You might choose to operate in more than one quadrant, and maybe in all four quadrants. We are all different, and one quadrant is not more important or better than another. In every village, town, city and nation in the world, there is a need for people operating in all four quadrants to ensure the financial stability of the community.

Also, as we grow older and gain different experiences, our interests change. For example, I notice that many young people right out of school are often happy to get a job. Yet, after a couple of years, a few of them decide they are not interested in climbing the corporate ladder, or they lose interest in the field of business they are in. These changes of age and experience often cause a person to search for new avenues of growth, challenge, financial reward and personal happiness. I hope this book offers some fresh ideas for attaining those goals.

In short, this book is not about homelessness but about finding a home . . . a home in a quadrant or quadrants.

CHAPTER TWO

Different Quadrants
. . . Different People

'You can't teach an old dog new tricks,' my highly educated dad always said.

I had sat with him on several occasions, doing my best to explain the *CASHFLOW Quadrant* in an effort to show him some new financial directions. Nearing 60 years of age, he was realizing that many of his dreams were not going to be fulfilled. His 'black-listing' seemed to go beyond the walls of the state government. He was now 'blacklisting' himself.

'I tried it, but it didn't work,' he said.

My dad was referring to his attempts to be successful in the 'S' quadrant with his own business as a self-employed consultant, and as a 'B' when he poured much of his life savings into a famous ice-cream franchise that failed.

Being bright, he conceptually understood the different technical skills required in each of the four quadrants. He knew he could learn them if he wanted to. But there was something else holding him back.

One day over lunch, I talked to my rich dad about my educated dad.

'Your father and I are not the same people at the core,' said rich dad. 'While we are both human beings, and we both have

25

fears, doubts, beliefs, strengths and weaknesses, we respond or handle those core similarities . . . differently.'

'Can you tell me the differences?' I asked.

'Not over one lunch,' said rich dad. 'But how we respond to those differences is what causes us to remain in one quadrant or another. When your dad tried to cross over from the "E" quadrant to the "B" quadrant, intellectually he could understand the process, but he couldn't handle it emotionally. When things did not go smoothly, and he began to lose money, he did not know what to do to solve the problems . . . so he went back to the quadrant he felt most comfortable in.'

'The "E" and sometimes "S" quadrant,' I said.

Rich dad nodded his head. 'When the fear of losing money and failing becomes too painful inside, a fear we both have, he chooses to seek security, and I choose to seek freedom.'

'And that is the core difference,' I said, signaling the waiter for our check.

'Even though we're all human beings,' restated rich dad, 'when it comes to money and the emotions attached to money, we all respond differently. And it's how we respond to those emotions that often determines which quadrant we choose to generate our income from.'

'Different quadrants . . . different people,' I said.

'That's right,' said rich dad as we stood and headed for the door. 'And if you're going to be successful in any quadrant, you need to know more than just technical skills. You also need to know the core differences that cause people to seek different quadrants. Know that, and life will be much easier.'

We were shaking hands and saying goodbye as the valet brought my rich dad's car around.

'Oh, one last thing,' I said hurriedly. 'Can my dad change?'

'Oh sure,' said rich dad. 'Anyone can change. But changing quadrants is not like changing jobs or changing professions.

Changing quadrants is often a change at the core of who you are, how you think, and how you look at the world. The change is easier for some people than for others simply because some people welcome change and others fight it. And changing quadrants is most often a life-changing experience. It is a change as profound as the age-old story of the caterpillar becoming a butterfly. Not only will you change but so will your friends. While you'll still be friends with your old friends, it's just harder for caterpillars to do the same things butterflies do. So the changes are big changes, and not too many people choose to make them.'

The valet closed the door, and as my rich dad drove off, I was left thinking about the differences.

What Are The Differences?

How do I tell if people are an 'E, S, B or I' without knowing much about them? One of the ways is by listening to their words.

One of my rich dad's greatest skills was being able to 'read' people, but he also believed you could not 'judge a book by its cover.' Rich dad, like Henry Ford, did not have an excellent education, but both men knew how to hire and work with people who did. Rich dad always explained to me that the ability to bring smart people together and work as a team was one of his primary skills.

From the age of 9, my rich dad began to teach me the skills necessary to be successful in the 'B' and 'I' quadrants. One of those skills was to get beyond the surface of a person and begin to gaze into their core. Rich dad used to say, 'If I listen to a person's words, I begin to see and feel their souls.'

So at the age of 9, I began to sit in with my rich dad when he hired people. From these interviews I learned to listen not so much for words but for core values. Values that my rich dad said came from their souls.

'E' Quadrant Words

A person who comes from the 'E,' or employee, quadrant might say:

> 'I am looking for a safe, secure job with good pay and excellent benefits.'

'S' Quadrant Words

A person who comes from the 'S,' or self-employed, quadrant might say:

> 'My rate is $35 per hour.'
>
> Or 'My normal commission rate is 6 percent of the total price.'
>
> Or 'I can't seem to find people who want to work and do the job right.'
>
> Or 'I've got more than 20 hours into this project.'

'B' Quadrant Words

A person operating out of the 'B,' or business-owner, quadrant might say:

> 'I'm looking for a new president to run my company.'

'I' Quadrant Words

Someone operating out of the 'I,' or investor, quadrant might say:

> 'Is my cash flow based on an internal rate of return or net rate of return?'

Words Are Tools

Once my rich dad knew who the person he was interviewing was at the core, at least for that moment, he would know what they were really looking for, what he had to offer, and what words to use when speaking to them. Rich dad always said, 'Words are powerful tools.'

Rich dad had constantly reminded his son and me of this. 'If you want to be a leader of people, then you need to be a master of words.'

So one of the skills necessary to be a great 'B' is to be a master of words, knowing which words work on which kinds of people. He trained us to first listen carefully to the words a person used, and then we would know which words we should use, and when to use them in order to respond to them in the most effective way.

Rich dad explained, 'One word may excite one type of person while that same word would completely turn off another person.'

For example, the word 'risk' might be exciting to a person in the 'I' quadrant, while evoking total fear to someone in the 'E' quadrant.

To be great leaders, rich dad stressed that we first had to be great listeners. If you did not listen to the words a person used, you would not be able to feel their soul. If you did not listen to their soul, you would never know to whom you were talking.

Core Differences

The reason he would say, 'Hear their words, feel their souls,' is because behind the words a person chooses are the core values and core differences of that individual. The following are some of the generalities that separate people in one quadrant from those in another.

1. *The 'E' (employee).* When I hear the word 'secure' or 'benefits,' I get a sense of who they might be at the core. The word 'secure' is a word often used in response to the emotion of fear. If a person feels fear, then the need for security is often

a commonly used phrase for someone who comes predominantly from the 'E' quadrant. When it comes to money and jobs, there are many people who simply hate the feeling of fear that comes with economic uncertainty . . . hence the desire for security.

The word 'benefit' means people would also like some kind of additional reward that is spelled out – a defined and assured extra compensation, such as a health-care or retirement plan. The key is that they want to feel secure and see it in writing. Uncertainty does not make them happy; certainty does. Their internal workings say, 'I'll give you this . . . and you promise to give me that in return.'

They want their fear satisfied with some degree of certainty, so they seek security and strong agreements when it comes to employment. They are accurate when they say, 'I'm not that interested in money.'

For them, the idea of security is often more important than money.

Employees can be presidents of companies or janitors of companies. It is not so much what they do, but the contractual agreement they have with the person or organization that hires them.

2. *The 'S' (self-employed).* These are people who want to: 'Be their own boss.' Or they like to: 'Do their own thing.'

I call this group the 'do-it-yourselfers.'

Often, when it comes to the subject of money, a hard core 'S' does not like to have his or her income be dependent on other people. In other words, if 'S's' work hard, they expect to get paid for their work. Those who are 'S's' do not like having the amount of money they earn dictated by someone else or by a group of people who might not work as hard as they do. If they work hard, pay them well. They also understand that if they do not work hard, then they don't deserve to be paid much. When it comes to money, they have fiercely independent souls.

The Emotion Of Fear

So while the 'E,' or employee, often will respond to the fear of not having money by seeking 'security,' the 'S' often will respond differently. The people in this quadrant respond to fear not by seeking security, but by taking control of the situation and doing it on their own. That is why I call the 'S' group the 'do-it-yourself' group. When it comes to fear and financial risk, they want to 'take the bull by the horns.'

In this group you find well-educated 'professionals' who spend years in school, such as doctors, lawyers and dentists.

Also in the 'S' group are people who took educational paths other than, or in addition to, traditional school. In this group are direct-commission salespeople – real estate agents, for instance – as well as small business owners such as retail shopkeepers, cleaners, restauranteurs, consultants, therapists, travel agents, car mechanics, plumbers, carpenters, preachers, electricians, hair stylists, and artists.

This group's favorite song would be either 'Nobody Does It Better,' or 'I Did It My Way.'

Self-employed people are often hard-core 'perfectionists.' They often want to do something exceptionally well. In their mind, they do not think anyone else does it better than they can do it, so they really do not trust anyone else to do it the way they like it . . . the way they think is the 'right way.' In many respects, they are true artists with their own style and methods of doing things.

And that is why we hire them. If you hire a brain surgeon, you want that brain surgeon to have had years of training and experience, but most importantly, you want this brain surgeon to be a perfectionist. The same goes for a dentist, hairstylist, marketing consultant, plumber, electrician, tarot-card reader, lawyer or a corporate trainer. You, as the client hiring this person, want someone who is the best.

For this group, money is not the most important thing about their work. Their independence, the freedom to do things their way, and to be respected as experts in their field, are much more important than mere money. When hiring them, it is best to tell them what you want done and then leave them alone to do it. They do not need or want supervision. If you meddle too much, they'll simply walk off the job and tell you to hire someone else. The money really does not come first; their independence does.

This group often has a hard time hiring other people to do what they do simply because in their mind, nobody is up to the task. Which causes this group to often say: 'It's hard to find good help these days.'

Also, if this group trains someone to do what they do, that newly trained person often ends up leaving to 'do their own thing,' and 'be their own boss,' and 'do things their way,' and 'to have a chance to express their individuality.'

Many 'S' types are hesitant to hire and train other people because once trained they often end up as their competition. This, in turn, keeps them working harder and doing things on their own.

3. *The 'B' (business owner).* This group of people could almost be the opposite of the 'S.' Those who are true 'B's' like to

surround themselves with smart people from all four categories, 'E, S, B and I.' Unlike the 'S,' who does not like to delegate work (because no one could do it better), the true 'B' likes to delegate. The true motto of a 'B' is, 'Why do it yourself when you can hire someone to do it for you, and they can do it better?'

Henry Ford fits this mold. As one popular story goes, a group of so-called intellectuals came by to condemn Ford for being 'ignorant.' They claimed he really did not know much. So Ford invited them into his office and challenged them to ask him any question and he would answer it. So this panel assembled around America's most powerful industrialist, and began to ask him questions. Ford listened to their questions, and when they were through, he simply reached for several phones on his desk and called in some of his bright assistants, and asked them to give the panel the answers they sought. He ended by informing the panel that he would rather hire smart people who went to school to come up with answers so he could leave his mind clear to do more important tasks. Tasks like 'thinking.'

One of the quotes credited to Ford goes: 'Thinking is the hardest work there is. That is why so few people engage in it.'

Leadership Is Bringing Out The Best In People

My rich dad's idol was Henry Ford. He had me read books about people like Ford and John D. Rockefeller, the founder of Standard Oil. Rich dad constantly encouraged his son and me to learn the essence of leadership and the technical skills of business. In retrospect, I understand now that many people may have one or the other, but to be a successful 'B,' you really do need to have both. I also now realize that both skills can be learned. There is a science to business and leadership as well as an art to business and leadership. For me, both are lifelong studies.

When I was a boy my rich dad gave me a children's book

entitled *Stone Soup*, written in 1947 by Marcia Brown and still available today from leading bookstores. He had me read this book to begin my training as a leader in business.

Leadership, rich dad said, is 'the ability to bring out the best in people.' So he trained his son and me in the technical skills necessary to become successful in business, technical skills such as reading financial statements, marketing, sales, accounting, management, production and negotiations, and he really stressed that we learn to work with and lead people. Rich dad always said, 'The technical skills of business are easy . . . the hard part is working with people.'

As a reminder, I still read *Stone Soup* today, for I personally have a tendency to be a tyrant, instead of a leader, when things do not go my way.

Enterpreneurial Development

I have often heard the words, 'I'm going to start my own business.'

Many people tend to believe that the way to financial security and happiness is to 'do your own thing,' or to 'develop a new product no one else has.'

So they rush out and start their own business. In many cases, this is the path they take.

Many wind up starting an 'S' type of business and not a 'B' type of business. Again, not that one is necessarily better than the other. Both have different strengths and weakness, risks and rewards. But many people who want to start a 'B' type of business wind up with an 'S' type of business and become stalled in their quest to move to the right side of the *Quadrant*.

Many new entrepreneurs want to do this:

But wind up instead doing this and getting stuck there.

Many then attempt to do this:

But only a few who attempt actually make it. Why? Because the technical skills and human skills to be successful in each quadrant are often different. You must learn the skills and mind-set required by a quadrant in order to find true success there.

The Difference Between An 'S' Type Of Business And A 'B' Type Of Business

Those who are true 'B's can leave their business for a year or more and return to find their business more profitable and running better than when they left it. In a true 'S' type of business, if the 'S' left for a year or more, the chances are there would be no business left to return to.

So what causes the difference? Saying it simply, an 'S' owns a job. A 'B' owns a system and then hires competent people to operate the system. Or put another way: In many cases, the 'S' is the system. That is why they cannot leave.

Let's take a dentist. A dentist spends years in school learning to become a self-contained system. You, as the client, get a toothache. You go see your dentist. He fixes your tooth.

You pay and go home. You're happy and then tell all of your friends about your great dentist. In most cases, the dentist can do the entire job by himself. The problem is that if the dentist goes on vacation, so does his income.

'B' business owners can go on vacation forever because they own a system, not a job. If the 'B' is on vacation, the money still comes in.

To be successful as a 'B' requires:

A. Ownership or control of systems, and
B. The ability to lead people.

For 'S's' to evolve into 'B's,' they need to convert who they are and what they know into a system . . . and many are not able to do that . . . or they are often too attached to the system.

Can You Make A Better Hamburger Than McDonald's?

Many people come to me for advice on how to start a company or to ask me how to raise money for a new product or idea.

I listen, usually for about 10 minutes, and within that time I can tell where their focus is. Is it the product or the system of business? In those 10 minutes, I most often hear words such as these (remember the importance of being a good listener and allowing words to direct you to the core values of a person's soul):

'This is a far better product than company XYZ makes.'

'I've looked everywhere, and nobody has this product.'

'I'll give you the idea for this product; all I want is 25 percent of the profits.'

'I've been working on this (product, book, music score, invention) for years.'

These are the words of a person generally operating from the left side of the *Quadrant*, the 'E' or 'S' side.

It is important to be gentle at this time, because we are dealing with core values and ideas that have been entrenched often for years . . . maybe handed down for generations. If I am not gentle or patient, I could damage a fragile and sensitive launch of an idea and, more importantly, a human being ready to evolve into another quadrant.

The Hamburger And The Business

Since I need to be gentle, at this point in the conversation I often use the 'McDonald's hamburger' example for clarification. After listening to their pitch, I slowly ask, 'Can you personally make a better hamburger than McDonald's?'

So far, 100 percent of the people I have talked with about their new idea or product have said 'yes.' They can all prepare, cook and serve a better quality hamburger than McDonald's.

At this point, I ask them the next question: 'Can you personally build a better business system than McDonald's?'

Some people see the difference immediately, and some do not. And I would say the difference is whether the person is fixated on the left side of the *Quadrant*, which is focused on the idea of the better burger, or on the right side of the *Quadrant*, which is focused on the system of business.

I do my best to explain that there are a lot of entrepreneurs out there offering far superior products or services than are offered by the mega-rich multinational corporations, just as there are billions of people who can make a better burger than McDonald's. But only McDonald's has the system that has served billions of burgers.

See The Other Side

If people can begin to see the other side, I then suggest they go to McDonald's, buy a burger, and sit and look at the system that delivered that burger. Take note of the trucks that delivered the raw burger, the rancher that raised the beef, the buyer who bought the beef, and the TV ads with Ronald McDonald. Notice the training of young inexperienced people to say the same words, 'Hello, welcome to McDonald's,' as well as the decor of the franchise, the regional offices, the bakeries that bake the buns, and the millions of pounds of French fries that taste exactly the same all over the world. Then include the stockbrokers raising money for McDonald's on Wall Street. If they can begin to understand the 'whole picture,' then they have a chance at moving to the 'B' or 'I' side of the *Quadrant.*

The reality is, there are unlimited new ideas, billions of people with services or products to offer, millions of products, and only a few people who know how to build excellent business systems.

Bill Gates of Microsoft did not build a great product. He bought somebody else's product and built a powerful global system around it.

4. *The 'I' (investor).* Investors make money with money. They do not have to work because their money is working for them.

The 'I' quadrant is the playground of the rich. Regardless of which quadrant people make their money in, if they hope someday to be rich, they ultimately must come to the 'I' quadrant. It is in the 'I' quadrant that money becomes converted to wealth.

The Cashflow Quadrant

That is the *CASHFLOW Quadrant*. The *Quadrant* simply makes distinctions on how income is generated, whether as an 'E' (employee), 'S' (self-employed), 'B' (business owner) or 'I' (investor). The differences are summarized below.

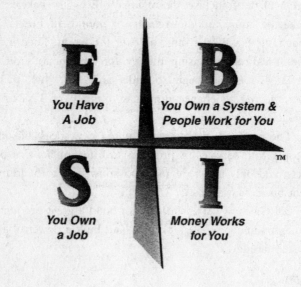

E You Have A Job

B You Own a System & People Work for You

S You Own a Job

I Money Works for You

OPT And OPM

Most of us have heard that the secrets to great riches and wealth are:

1. OPT – Other People's Time.
2. OPM – Other People's Money.

OPT and OPM are found on the right side of the *Quadrant*. For the most part, people who work on the left side of the *Quadrant* are the OP (Other People) whose time and money are being used.

A primary reason Kim and I took time to build a 'B' type of business, rather than an 'S' type, was because we recognized the long-term benefit of using 'other people's time'. One of the drawbacks to being a successful 'S' is that success simply means more hard work. In other words, good work results in more hard work and longer hours.

In designing a 'B' type of business, success simply means increasing the system and hiring more people. In other words, you work less, earn more and enjoy more free time.

The remainder of this book goes through the skills and mind-set required for the right side of the *Quadrant*. It is my experience that being successful on the right side requires a different mind-set and different technical skills. If people are flexible enough to make a mind-set change, I think they will find the process of achieving greater financial security or freedom easy. For other people, the process might be too difficult . . . because many people are frozen in one quadrant, one mind-set.

At a minimum, you will find out why some people work less, earn more, pay less in taxes, and feel more financially secure than others. It is simply a matter of knowing which quadrant to work out of and when.

A Guide To Freedom

The CASHFLOW Quadrant is not a set of rules. It is only a guide for those who wish to use it. It guided Kim and me from financial struggle to financial security, and then to financial freedom. We did not want to spend every day of our lives having to get up and work for money.

The Difference Between The Rich And Everyone Else

A few years ago, I read this article that said most rich people received 70 percent of their income from investments, or the 'I' quadrant, and less than 30 percent from wages, or the 'E' quadrant. And if they were an 'E,' the chances were that they were employees of their own corporation.

Their income looked like this:

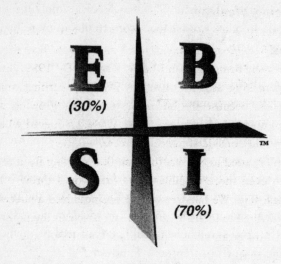

For most everyone else, the poor and the middle class, at least 80 percent of their income comes from wages from the 'E' or 'S' quadrants and less than 20 percent from investments, or the 'I' quadrant.

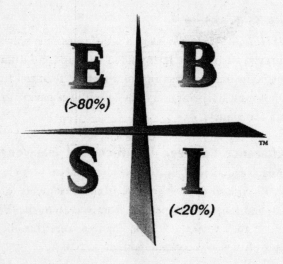

The Difference Between Being Rich And Being Wealthy

In Chapter 1, I wrote that my wife and I were millionaires by 1989, but we were not financially free until 1994. There is a difference between being rich and being wealthy. By 1989, our business was making us a lot of money. We were earning more and working less because the business system was growing without any more physical effort on our part. We had achieved what most people would consider financial success.

We still needed to convert the cash flow coming from the business into even more tangible assets that would throw off additional cash flow. We had grown our business into a success, and it was now time to focus on growing our assets to the point where the cash flow from all of our assets would be greater than our living expenses.

Our diagram looked like this:

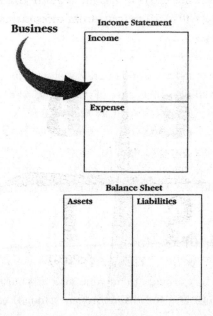

By 1994, the passive income from all of our assets was greater than our expenses. Then, we were wealthy.

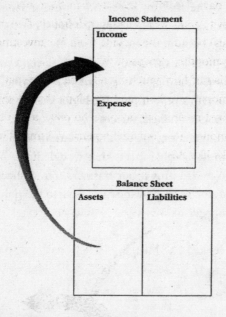

Income Statement

Income

Expense

Balance Sheet

Assets | Liabilities

In actuality, our business would also be considered an asset because it generated income and operated without much physical input. For our own personal sense of wealth, we wanted to make sure we had tangible assets such as real estate and stocks that were throwing off more passive income than our expenses, so we could really say we were wealthy. Once the income from our asset column was greater than the money coming in from the business, we sold the business to our partner. We were now wealthy.

The Definition Of Wealth

The definition of wealth is: 'The number of days you can survive, without physically working (or anyone else in your household physically working) and still maintain your standard of living.'

For example: If your monthly expenses are $1,000 a month, and if you have $3,000 in savings, your wealth is approximately 3 months or 90 days. Wealth is measured in time, not dollars.

By 1994, my wife and I were wealthy indefinitely (barring great economic changes) because the income from our investments was greater than our monthly expenses.

Ultimately, it is not how much money you make that matters, but how much money you keep and how long that money works for you. Every day I meet many people who make a lot of money, but all of their money goes out the expense column. Their cash flow pattern looks like this:

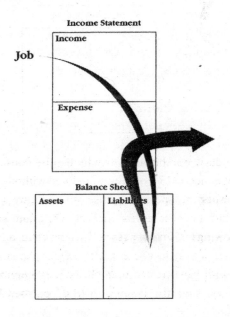

Every time they make a little more money, they go shopping. They often buy a bigger house or new car, which results in long-term debt and more hard work, and nothing is left to go into the asset column. The money goes out so fast, you'd think they took some kind of financial laxative.

Red Line Finances

In the world of cars, there is a saying about 'keeping the engine at red line.' 'Red line' means the throttle is keeping the RPMs of the engine as close to the 'red line,' or the maximum speed the car's engine can maintain, without blowing up.

When it comes to personal finances, there are many people, rich and poor, who operate constantly at the financial 'red line.' No matter how much money they make, they spend it as fast as it comes in. The trouble with operating your car's engine at 'red line' is that the life expectancy of the engine is shortened. The same is true with operating your finances at the 'red line.'

Several of my medical doctor friends say the main problem they see today is stress caused by working hard and never having enough money. One says that the biggest cause of health disorders is something she calls, 'cancer of the wallet.'

Money Making Money

Regardless of how much money people make, ultimately they should put some in the 'I' quadrant. The 'I' quadrant deals specifically with the idea of money making money. Or the idea that your money works so that you do not have to work. Yet it is important to acknowledge that there are other forms of investing.

Other Forms Of Investing

People invest in their education. Traditional education is important because the better your education, the better your chances of earning money. You can spend four years in college and have your income earning potential go from $24,000 a year to $50,000 a year or more. Given that the average person spends 40 years or more actively working, four years' worth of college or some type of higher education is an excellent investment.

Loyalty and hard work is another form of investing, like being a lifelong employee of a company or the government. In return, via contract, that individual is rewarded with a pension for life. That is a form of investment popular in the Industrial Age but obsolete in the Information Age.

Other people invest in having large families and, in turn, have their children care for them in their old age. That form of investing was the norm in the past, yet due to economic constraints in the present, it is becoming more difficult for families to handle the living and medical expenses of parents.

Government retirement programs such as Social Security and Medicare in America, which are often paid for through payroll deduction, is another form of investment mandated by law. But due to massive changes in demographics and costs, this form of investment may not be able to keep some of the promises it has made.

And there are independent investment vehicles for retirement that are called individual retirement plans. Often, the federal government will offer tax incentives to both the employer and employee to participate in such plans. In America, one popular plan is the 401(k) retirement plan, and in countries such as Australia, they are called 'Superannuation' plans.

Income Received From Investments

Although the above are all forms of investing, the 'I' quadrant focuses on investments that generate income on an ongoing basis during your working years. So to qualify as a person who operates as an 'I,' use the same criteria used in all the other quadrants. Do you receive current income from the 'I' quadrant? In other words, is your money working for you and generating current income for you?

Let's look at a person who buys a house as an investment and rents it out. If the rent collected is greater than the expenses to operate the property, that income is coming from the 'I' quadrant. The same is true for people who receive income as interest from savings, or dividends from stocks and bonds. So the qualifier for the 'I' quadrant is how much income you generate from the quadrant without working in it.

Is My Retirement Account A Form Of Investment?

Regularly putting money into a retirement account is a form of investing and is a wise thing to do. Most of us hope to be considered investors when our working years are over . . . but for the sake of this book, the 'I' quadrant represents a person whose income comes from investments during their working years. In reality, most people are not investing in a retirement account. Most are saving money in their retirement account, hoping that, when they reitre, there will be more money coming out than they put in.

There is a difference between people who save money in their retirement accounts and people who, through investing, actively use their money to make more money as income.

Are Stockbrokers Investors?

Many people who are advisers in the investment world are, by definition, not really people who generate their income from the 'I' quadrant.

For example, most stockbrokers, real estate agents, financial advisers, bankers and accountants are predominantly 'E's' or 'S's.' In other words, their income comes from their professional work, not necessarily from assets they own.

I also have friends who are stock traders. They buy stocks low and hope to sell high. In reality, their profession is 'trading,' much like a person who owns a retail shop and buys items at wholesale and sells them at retail. There is still something they physically must do to generate the money. So they would fit more into the 'S' quadrant than the 'I' quadrant.

Can all of these people be investors? The answer is 'yes,' but it is important to know the difference between someone who earns money from commissions, or sells advice by the hour, or gives advice for a salary, or tries to buy low and sell high, and someone who earns money from spotting or creating good investments.

There's one way to find out how good your advisers are: Ask them what percentage of their income comes from commissions or fees for their advice vs. income that comes from passive income, income from their investments or other businesses they own.

I have several CPA friends who tell me, without violating client confidentiality, that many professional investment advisers have little in the way of income from investments. In other words, 'They do not practice what they preach.'

Advantages Of Income From The 'I' Quadrant

So the primary distinction of people who earn their money from the 'I' quadrant is that they focus on having their money make money. If they are good at it, they can have that money work for them and for their family for hundreds of years.

Besides the obvious advantages of knowing how to make money with money and not having to get up and go to work, there also are many tax advantages that are not available to people who have to work for their money.

One of the reasons the rich get richer is because they sometimes can make millions and legally not pay taxes on that money. That's because they make money in the 'asset column,' not in the 'income column.' Or they make money as investors, not workers.

For people who work for money, not only are they often taxed at higher rates, their taxes are withheld from their wages and they never even see that portion of their income.

Why Aren't More People Investors?

The 'I' quadrant is the quadrant for working less, earning more, and paying less in taxes. So why aren't more people investors?

The same reason many people do not start their own businesses. It can be summed up in one word: 'risk.'

Many people do not like the idea of handing over their hard earned money and not having it come back. Many people are so afraid of losing, they choose not to invest or risk their money at all . . . no matter how much money they could make in return.

A Hollywood celebrity once said: 'It's not return on the investment that I worry about. It's the return of the investment.'

This fear of losing money seems to divide investors into four broad categories:

1. People who are risk-adverse and do nothing but play it safe, keeping their money in the bank.
2. People who turn the job of investing over to someone else, such as a financial adviser or mutual fund manager.
3. Gamblers.
4. Investors.

The difference between a gambler and an investor is this. For a gambler, investing is a game of chance. For an investor, investing is a game of skill. And for the people who turn their money over to someone else to invest, investing is often a game they do not want to learn. The important thing for these individuals is to choose a financial adviser carefully.

In an upcoming chapter, this book will go into the seven levels of investors, which should shed more light on this subject.

Risk Can Be Virtually Eliminated

The good news about investing is that risk can be greatly minimized or even eliminated, and you can still receive high yields on your money, if you know the game.

A true investor will be heard speaking these words: 'How soon do I get my money back and how much income will I receive for the rest of my life after I get that initial investment money back?'

A true investor wants to know how soon they get their money back. People who have a retirement account have to wait years to find out if they will ever get their money back. This is the most extreme difference between a professional investor and someone who sets money aside for retirement.

It is the fear of losing money that causes most people to seek security. Yet the 'I' quadrant is not as treacherous as many people think. The 'I' quadrant is like any other quadrant. It has its own skills and mind-set. The skills to be successful in the 'I' quadrant can be learned if you're willing to take the time to learn them.

A New Age Begins

In 1989, the Berlin Wall came down. In the history of the world, that was one of the most important events. More than signifying the failure of communism, in my opinion, that event marked the official end of the Industrial Age and the beginning of the Information Age.

The Difference Between Industrial-age Pension Plans And Information-age Pension Plans

The voyage of Columbus in 1492 roughly coincides with the start of the Industrial Age. The fall of the Berlin Wall in 1989 is the event that marked the end of that age. For some reason, it seems that every 500 years in modern history, great cataclysmic changes have occurred. We are in one such period right now.

That change has already threatened the financial security of hundreds of millions of people, most of whom are not yet aware of the financial impact of that change and many of whom cannot afford it. The change is found in the difference between an Industrial Age pension plan and an Information Age pension plan.

When I was a boy, my rich dad encouraged me to take risks

with my money and learn to invest. He would always say: 'If you want to get rich, you need to learn how to take risks. Learn to be an investor.'

At home, I told my educated dad about my rich dad's suggestion that we learn how to invest and learn to manage risk. My educated dad replied, 'I don't need to learn how to invest. I have a government pension plan, a pension from the Teachers Union, and Social Security benefits guaranteed. Why take risks with my money?'

My educated dad believed in Industrial Age pension plans, such as government-employee pensions and Social Security. He was happy when I signed up for the U.S. Marine Corps. Instead of being worried that I might lose my life in Vietnam, he simply said, 'Stay in for 20 years and you will get a pension and medical benefits for life.'

Although still in use, such pension plans officially have become obsolete. The idea of a company being financially responsible for your retirement and the government picking up the balance of your retirement needs through pension schemes is an old idea that is no longer valid.

People Need To Become Investors

As we move from Defined Benefit pension plans, or what I call Industrial Age retirement plans, to Defined Contribution pension plans, or Information Age pension plans, the result is that you as an individual must now be financially responsible for yourself. Few people have noticed the change.

Industrial Age Pension Plan

In the Industrial Age, a Defined Benefit pension plan meant that the company guaranteed you, the worker, a defined amount of money (usually paid monthly) for as long as you lived. People felt secure because these plans assured a steady income.

Information Age Pension Plan

Somebody changed the deal, and companies suddenly were no longer guaranteeing financial security at the end of your working days. Instead, companies began offering Defined Contribution retirement plans. 'Defined Contribution' means that you are only going to get back what you and the company have contributed while you were working. In other words, your pension is defined solely by what has been contributed. If you and your company put no money in, you get no money out.

The good news is that in the Information Age, life expectancy will go up. The bad news is that you might outlive your pension.

Risky Pension Plans

And worse than that, what you and your employer put into the plan is no longer guaranteed to exist when you decide to pull it out. This is because plans like 401(k)s and Superannuations, are subject to market forces. In other words, one day you could have a million dollars in the account, and if there were a stock-market crash, which every market occasionally has, your million dollars could be cut in half or even wiped out. The guarantee of lifelong income is gone . . . and I wonder how many people who have these plans realize what this means.

It could mean that people who retire at 65, and begin to live on their Defined Contribution plan, could run out of money by, let's say, age 75. Then, what do they do? Dust off the resume.

And what about the government's Defined Benefit pension plan? Well, in the United States, Social Security is expected to be bankrupt by the year 2032 and Medicare bankrupt by 2005, just when baby boomers begin needing it. Even today, Social Security does not provide much in the way of income. What will happen when 77 million baby boomers begin to want the money they paid in . . . but it's not there?

In 1998, President Clinton's popular cry of 'Save Social Security' was well received. Yet as Democratic Senator Ernest Hollings pointed out, 'Obviously the first way to save Social Security is to stop looting it.' For decades, the federal government has been responsible for 'borrowing' the retirement money for expenditures.

Many politicians seem to think that Social Security is income that can be spent rather than an asset that should be held in trust.

Too Many People Counting On The Government

I write my books and build my products, such as the educational board game *CASHFLOW*, because we are at the end of the Industrial Age and just getting started in the Information Age.

My concern as a private citizen is that from my generation forward, we are not properly prepared to handle the differences between the Industrial Age and the Information Age . . . and one of those differences is how we prepare financially for our retirement years. The idea of 'go to school and get a safe, secure job' was a good idea for people born before 1930. Today, everyone needs to go to school to learn to get a good job, but we also need to know how to invest, and investing is not a subject taught in school.

One of the hangovers of the Industrial Age is that too many people have become dependent on the government to solve their individual problems. Today we are facing even bigger problems because of the delegation to the government of our personal financial responsibility.

It is estimated that by the year 2020, there will be 275 million Americans, with 100 million of them expecting some kind of government support. This will include federal employees, military retirees, postal workers, schoolteachers and other government employees, as well as retirees expecting Social Security and Medicare payments. And they are contractually correct in expecting it because, in one way or another, most have been investing in that promise. Unfortunately, there have been too many promises made for years, and now the bill is coming due.

And I do not think those financial promises can be kept. If our government begins to raise taxes even higher to pay for those promises, those who can escape will escape to countries that have lower taxes. In the Information Age, the term 'offshore' will not mean another country as a tax haven . . . 'offshore' could mean 'cyberspace.'

A Great Change Is At Hand

I recall President John F. Kennedy warning, 'A great change is at hand.'

Well, that change is here.

Investing Without Being Investors

The change from Defined Benefit to Defined Contribution pension plans is forcing millions of people throughout the world to become investors, with little investor education. Many people who have spent their lives avoiding financial risks are now being forced to take them . . . financial risks with their future, their old age, the end of their working years. Most will find out if they were wise investors or careless gamblers only when it comes time to retire.

Today, the stock market is the talk of the world. It is fueled by many things, one of which is non-investors trying to become investors. Their financial path looks like this:

A large majority of these people, the 'E's' and 'S's,' are people who by nature are security oriented. That is why they seek secure jobs or secure careers, or start small business they can control. They are migrating today, because of the Defined Contribution retirement plans, to the 'I' quadrant, where they hope they will find 'security' for when their working years are over. Unfortunately, the 'I' quadrant is not known for its security. The 'I' quadrant is the quadrant of risk.

Because so many people on the left side of the *CASHFLOW Quadrant* come looking for security, the stock market responds in kind. That is why you hear so often the following words:

1. 'Diversification.' People who seek security use the word 'diversification' a lot. Why? Because the strategy of diversification is an investment strategy for 'not losing.' It is not an investment strategy for winning. Successful or rich investors do not diversify. They focus their efforts.

   Warren Buffett, possibly the world's greatest investor, says this about 'diversification': 'The strategy we've adopted precludes our following standard diversification dogma. Many pundits would therefore say the strategy must be riskier than that employed by more conventional investors. We disagree. We believe that a policy of portfolio concentration may well decrease risk if it raises, as it should, both the intensity with which an investor thinks about a business and the comfort level he must feel with its economic characteristics before buying into it.'

   In other words, Warren Buffett is saying that portfolio concentration or focusing on a few investments, rather than diversifying, is a better strategy. In his mind, concentration rather than diversification requires you to become smarter, more intense in your thoughts and actions. His article goes on to say that average investors avoid volatility because they think volatility is risky. Warren Buffet says instead, 'In fact, the true investor welcomes volatility.'

For my wife and me to get out of financial struggle and find financial freedom, we did not diversify. We concentrated our investments.

2. 'Blue Chip Stocks.' Security-minded investors usually buy 'Blue Chip' companies. Why? Because in their mind, they are safer. While the company might be safer, the stock market is not.

3. 'Mutual Funds.' People who know little about investing feel more secure about turning their money over to a fund manager they hope will do a better job than they can. And this is a smart strategy for people who have no intention of becoming professional investors. The problem is, as smart as this strategy is, it does not mean that mutual funds are less risky. In fact, if there is a stock-market crash, we might see what I call the 'Mutual Fund Meltdown,' a financial catastrophe as devastating as the 'Tulipomania' crash in 1610, the 'South Seas Bubble' meltdown of 1620, and the 'Junk Bond' bombshell of 1990.

Today, the market is filled with millions of people who, by nature, are security minded, but due to the changing economy are being forced to cross from the left side of the *CASHFLOW Quadrant* into the right side, where their brand of security does not really exist. That causes me concern. Many people think their pension plans are safe, when they really are not. If there is a crash or a major depression, their plans could be wiped out. Their retirement plans are not as safe as the retirement plans our parents had.

Great Economic Upheavals Coming
The stage is set for a great economic upheaval. Such upheavals have always marked the end of an old era and the birth of a new

era. At the end of every age there are people who move forward and other people who cling to ideas of the past. I am afraid that for people who still expect that their financial security is the responsibility of a big company or big government, they will be disappointed in the coming years. Those are ideas of the Industrial Age, not the Information Age.

No one has a crystal ball. I subscribe to many investment news services. Each one says something different. Some say the near future is bright. Some say a market crash and major depression are right around the corner. To remain objective, I listen to both sides, because both sides have points worth listening to. The tack I take is not one of playing fortuneteller and trying to predict the future; instead I work at staying educated in both the 'B' and 'I' quadrants and being prepared for whatever happens. A person who is prepared will prosper no matter which direction the economy goes, whenever it goes.

If history is any indicator, a person who lives to the age of 75 should anticipate going through one depression and two major recessions. Well, my parents went through their depression, but the baby boomers have not . . . yet. And it has been approximately 60 years since the last depression hit.

Today we all need to be concerned with more than just job security. I think we also need to be concerned about our own long-term financial security . . . and not leave that responsibility to a company or the government. The times officially changed when companies said that they were no longer responsible for your retirement years. Once they switched to the Defined Contribution retirement plan, the message was that you were now responsible for investing in your own retirement. Today, we all need to become wiser investors, ever vigilant of the changes in the ups and downs of the financial markets. I recommend learning to be an investor rather than giving your money to somebody else to invest for you. If you simply turn your money over to a mutual fund or to an adviser, you may have to wait until you're 65 to find out if that person did a good job. If they did a lousy job, you may have to work for the rest of your life. Millions of people will have to do just that because it will be too late for them to invest or learn about investing.

Learn To Manage Risk

It is possible to invest for high returns with low risk. All you have to do is learn how it's done. It is not hard. In fact, it's much like learning how to ride a bike. In the early stages, you may fall down, but after a while, the falling stops and investing becomes second nature, just as riding a bicycle is for most of us.

The problem with the left side of the *CASHFLOW Quadrant* is that most people go there to avoid financial risk. Instead of avoiding risk, I recommend learning how to manage financial risk.

Take A Risk

People who take risks change the world. Few people ever get rich without taking risks. Too many people have come to depend on government to eliminate the risks of life. The beginning of the Information Age is the end of big government as we know it. Big government has just become too expensive. Unfortunately, the millions of people around the world that have come to depend upon the idea of 'entitlements' and pensions for life will be left behind financially. The Information Age means we all need to become more self-sufficient and begin to grow up.

The idea of 'study hard and find a safe, secure job' is an idea born in the Industrial Age. We're not in that age anymore. The times are changing. The problem is many people's ideas have not. They still think they're entitled to something. Many still think that the 'I' quadrant is not their responsibility. They continue to think that the government or a big business or the labor union or their mutual fund or their family will take care of them when their working days are over. For their sake, I hope they're right. These individuals have no need to read farther.

It is my concern for those people who recognize the need to become investors that prompted me to write *The CASHFLOW Quadrant*. It was written to help individuals who want to make the move from the left side of the *Quadrant* to the right side, but don't know where to start. Anyone can make the move with the right skills and determination.

If you have already found your own financial freedom, I say, 'Congratulations.' Please tell others about your path, and guide them if they want to be guided. Guide them, but let them find their own path, for there are many paths to financial freedom.

Regardless of what you decide, please remember this. Financial freedom might be free, but it does not come cheap. Freedom has a price . . . and to me it is worth the price. The big secret is this: It takes neither money to be financially free nor a good formal education. It also doesn't have to be risky. Instead, freedom's price is measured in dreams, desire and the ability to overcome disappointments that occur to all of us along the way. Are you willing to pay the price?

One of my fathers paid the price; the other didn't. He paid a different kind of price.

The B Quadrant Quiz

Are you a true business owner?

You are if you can answer 'YES' to the following question:

Can you leave your business for a year or more and return to find it more profitable and running better than when you left it?

☐ **Yes**　　☐ **No**

CHAPTER THREE

Why People Choose Security Over Freedom

Both of my dads recommended that I go to college and get a college degree. But it was after receiving the degree that their advice to me changed.

My highly educated dad constantly advised: 'Go to school, get good grades, and then get a good safe, secure job.'

He was recommending a life path focused on the left side of the *Quadrant* that looked like this.

My uneducated but rich dad advised focusing on the right side of the *Quadrant*: 'Go to school, get good grades, and then start your own company.'

Their advice was different because one dad was concerned with job security, and the other was more concerned about financial freedom.

Why People Seek Job Security

The primary reason many people seek job security is because that is what they are taught to seek, at home and at school.

Millions of people continue to follow that advice. Many of us have been conditioned from our earliest days to think about job security, rather than financial security or financial freedom. And because most of us learn little to nothing about money at home or at school, it is only natural that many of us cling even more tightly to the idea of job security . . . instead of reaching for freedom.

If you look at the *CASHFLOW Quadrant*, you will notice that the left side is motivated by security, and the right side is motivated by freedom.

Trapped By Debt

The main reason that 90 percent of the population is working on the left side is simply because that is the side they learn about at school. They then leave school and are soon deeply in debt. So deeply in debt that they must cling even tighter to a job, or professional security, just to pay the bills.

Often I meet young people who receive their college diploma along with the bill for their college loans. Several of them have reported being depressed when they see that they are $50,000 to $150,000 in debt for their college education. If the parents paid for their education, then the parents are strapped financially for years.

I recently read that most Americans today will receive a credit card while still in school and will be in debt for the rest of their lives. That is because they are often following a script that became popular in the Industrial Age.

Following The Script

If we track the life of average educated people, the financial script often goes like this:

The child goes to school, graduates, finds a job and soon has some money to spend. The young adult now can afford to rent an apartment, buy a TV set, new clothes, some furniture and, of course, a car. And now the bills begin to come in. One day, the adult meets someone special, sparks fly, they fall in love and get married. For a while, life is blissful because two can live as cheaply one. They now have two incomes, only one rent to pay, and they can afford to set a few dollars aside to buy the dream of all young couples, their own home. They find their dream home, pull the money from savings and use it for a down payment on the house, and they now have a mortgage. Because they have a new house, they need new furnishings, so they find a furniture store that advertises those magic words, 'No money down, easy monthly payments.'

Life is wonderful, and they throw a party to have all their friends over to see their new house, new car, new furniture, and new toys. They are now deeply in debt for the rest of their lives. Then, the first child arrives.

The average well-educated, hard-working couple, after dropping the child off at nursery school, must now put their nose to the grindstone and go to work. They become trapped by the need for job security simply because, on average, they are less than three months away from financial bankruptcy. From these people you often hear, 'I can't afford to quit. I have bills to pay,' or a modification from a song from Snow White and the Seven Dwarfs, 'I owe, I owe, so it's off to work I go.'

The Success Trap

One of the reasons I learned so much from my rich dad was because he had the free time to teach me. As he grew more successful, he had more free time and money. If business got better, he did not have to work harder. He simply had his president expand the system and hire more people to do the work. If his investments did well, he reinvested the money and made more money. Because of his success, he had more free time. He spent hours with both his son and me explaining to us everything he was doing in business and investing. I was learning more from him than I was learning at school. That is what happens when you work hard on the right side of the *Quadrant*, the 'B' and 'I' side.

My highly educated dad worked hard also, but he worked hard on the left side of the *Quadrant*. By working hard, getting promoted and gaining more responsibility, he had less and less free time to spend with his kids. He would leave for work at 7 a.m., and many times we would not see him because we had to go to bed before he got home. That is what happens when you work hard and become successful on the left side of the *Quadrant*. Success brings you less and less time . . . even if it does bring more money.

The Money Trap

Success on the right side of the *Quadrant* requires a knowledge about money called 'financial intelligence.' Rich dad defined it this way: 'Financial intelligence is not so much how much money you make, but how much money you keep, how hard that money works for you, and how many generations you keep it for.'

Success on the right side of the *Quadrant* requires financial intelligence. If people lack basic financial intelligence, they will, in most cases, not survive on the right side of the *Quadrant*.

My rich dad was good with money and with people at work. He had to be. He was responsible for creating money, managing as few people as possible, keeping costs low, and keeping profits high. Those are the skills necessary for success on the right side of the *Quadrant*.

It was my rich dad who stressed to me that your home is not an asset but a liability. He could prove it because he taught us to be financially literate so we were able to read numbers. He had the free time to teach his son and me because he was good at managing people. His skills from work carried over into his home life.

My educated dad did not manage money and people at work, although he thought he did. As the state Superintendent of Education, he was a government official with a multimillion dollar budget and thousands of employees. But it was not money he created. It was taxpayers' money, and his job was to spend all of it. If he did not spend it, the government would give him less money the next year. So at the end of each fiscal year, he was looking for ways to spend it all, which meant he often hired more people to justify next year's budget. The funny thing was, the more people he hired, the more problems he had.

As a young boy, observing both fathers, I began to take mental notes of what kind of life I wanted to lead.

My educated dad was a voracious reader of books, so he was word literate, but he was not financially literate. Because he could not read numbers, he had to take the advice of his banker and accountant, and both told him that his house was an asset, and that it should be his largest investment.

Because of this financial advice, not only did my highly educated dad work harder, but he also got further into debt. Every time he received a promotion for his hard work, he also got a pay raise, and with each pay raise he went into a higher tax bracket. Because he was in a higher tax bracket, and taxes for high-income workers in the 1960s and 1970s were extremely high, his accountant and banker would tell him to buy a bigger house so he could write off the interest payments. He made more money, but all that happened was his taxes increased and his debt increased. The more successful he got, the harder he had to work, and the less time he had with the people he loved. Soon, all the children were gone from home, and he was still working hard just to keep up with the bills.

He always thought that the next promotion and pay raise would solve his problem. But the more money he made, the more the same things happened. He got deeper into debt and paid more in taxes.

The more frazzled he got, both at home and at work, the more he seemed to depend on job security. The more emotionally attached he got to his job, and a paycheck to pay the bills, the more he encouraged his kids to 'get a safe, secure job.'

The more insecure he felt, the more he sought security.

Your Two Biggest Expenses

Because my dad could not read financial statements, he could not see the money trap he was getting into as he grew more successful. It's the same money trap I see millions of other successful hard-working people fall into.

The reason so many people struggle financially is because every time they make more money, they also increase their two biggest expenses:

1. Taxes.
2. Interest on debt.

To top it off, the government often offers you tax breaks to get deeper into debt. Doesn't that make you a little suspicious?

As my rich dad defined financial intelligence: 'It's not so much how much you make, but how much you keep, how hard it works for you, and how many generations you keep it for.'

At the end of my hard-working educated dad's life, the little money he did have to pass on . . . was taken by the government in probate taxes.

The Search For Freedom

I know many people search for freedom and happiness. The problem is most people have not been trained to work from the

'B' and 'I' quadrants. Because of this lack of training, the program-ming into job security, and their increasing amount of debt, most people limit their search for financial freedom to the left side of the *CASHFLOW Quadrant*. Unfortunately, financial security or financial freedom are seldom found in the 'E' or 'S' quadrant. True security and freedom are found on the right side.

Going From Job To Job In Search Of Freedom

One thing the *CASHFLOW Quadrant* is useful for is to track or observe a person's life pattern. Many people spend their life in search of security or freedom, but wind up instead going from job to job. For example:

I have a friend from high school. I hear from him about every five years, and he is always excited because he has found the perfect job. He is ecstatic because he has found the company of his dreams. He loves the company. It's doing exciting things. He loves his work, he has an important title, the pay is great, the people are great, the benefits are great, and his chances for promo-tion are great. About four and a half years later, I hear from him again, and by this time, he is dissatisfied. The company he works for is now corrupt and dishonest, in his opinion; it doesn't treat its workers with respect; he hates his boss; he was passed over for a promotion, and they don't pay him enough. Six months go by and he's happy again. He's ecstatic because he's found the perfect job . . . again.

His life's path looks something like a dog chasing its tail. It looks like this.

His life pattern is going from job to job. So far, he lives well because he is smart, attractive and personable. But the years are catching up with him, and younger people are now getting the jobs he used to get. He has a few thousand dollars in savings, nothing set aside for retirement, a house he will never own, child support payments, and college yet to pay for. His youngest child, 8, lives with his ex-wife, and his oldest child, 14, lives with him.

He used to always say to me, 'I don't have to worry. I'm still young. I have time.'

I wonder if he's saying that now.

In my opinion, he needs to make a serious effort to begin moving to either the 'B' or the 'I' quadrant quickly. A new attitude and a new educational process need to begin. Unless he gets lucky and wins the lottery, or finds a rich woman to marry, he is on a course of working hard for the rest of his life.

Doing Your Own Thing

'E's' Become 'S's'

Another common pattern is someone going from 'E' to 'S.' During this current period of massive downsizing, many people are getting the message and are leaving their jobs with big companies to start their own businesses. There is a boom in so-called 'home-based businesses.' So many people made the decision to 'Start their own business,' 'Do their own thing' and 'Be their own boss.'

Their career path looks like this.

Of all the life paths, this is the one I feel for the most. In my opinion, being an 'S' can be the most rewarding and also the most risky. I think the 'S' quadrant is the hardest quadrant there is. The failure rates are high. And if you make it, being successful can be worse than failing. That is because if you are successful as an 'S,' you will work harder than if you were in any of the other quadrants . . . and you will work harder for a long time. For as long as you are successful.

The reason 'S's' work the hardest is because they typically are the proverbial 'chief cook and bottle washer.' They have to do or be responsible for all the jobs that in a bigger company are done by many managers and employees. An 'S' just starting out often answers the phone, pays the bills, makes sales calls, tries to advertise on a small budget, handles customers, hires employees, fires employees, fills in when employees do not show up, talks to the tax man, fights off the government inspectors, and on and on.

Personally I cringe whenever I hear someone say they're going to start their own business. I wish them well, yet I feel great concern for them. I have seen so many 'E's' take their life savings or borrow money from friends and family to start their own business. After three or so years of struggle and hard work, the business folds, and instead of life savings, they have debt to pay off.

Nationally, nine out of 10 of these types of businesses fail in five years. Of the one that is remaining, nine out of 10 of them fail in the next five years. In other words, 99 out of 100 small businesses ultimately disappear in 10 years.

I think the reason most fail in the first five years is due to the lack of experience and lack of capital. The reason the one survivor often fails in the second five years is not due to lack of capital, but lack of energy. The hours of long, hard work finally get to the person. Many 'S's' just burn out. That is why so many highly educated professionals change firms or try to start something new, or die. Maybe that is why the average life expectancy for doctors and lawyers is lower than it is for most others. Their average life expectancy is 58. For everyone else, it is in the 70s.

For those who do survive, they seem to have become used to the idea of getting up, going to work and working hard forever. That seems to be all they know.

A friend's parents remind me of this. For 45 years they have spent long hours in their liquor store on a street corner. As crime increased in their neighborhood, they had to put steel bars up on the doors and all the windows. Today, money is passed through a slot, much like in a bank. I go by occasionally to see them. They are wonderful, sweet people, but it saddens me to see them as virtual prisoners in their own business, from 10 in the morning until 2 the next morning, staring out from behind the bars.

Many wise 'S's' sell their businesses at their peak, before they run out of steam, to someone with energy and money. They take some time off, and then start something new. They keep doing their own thing and love it. But they have to know when to get out.

The Worst Advice To Give Your Children

If you were born prior to 1930, the advice 'Go to school, get good grades, and find a safe, secure job' was good advice. But if you were born after 1930, it is bad advice.

Why?

The answer is found in: 1. Taxes. 2. Debt.

For people who earn their income out of the 'E' quadrant, there are virtually no tax breaks left. Today in America, being an employee means you are a 50/50 partner with the government. That means the government ultimately will take 50 percent or more of an employee's earnings, and much of that even before the employee sees the paycheck.

When you consider that the government offers you tax breaks for going further into debt, the path to financial freedom is virtually impossible for most people in the 'E' quadrant and for most in the 'S' Quadrant. I often hear accountants tell clients who begin earning more income from the 'E' quadrant to buy a bigger house so they can receive a bigger tax break. While that might make sense to someone on the left side of the *CASHFLOW Quadrant*, that makes no sense to someone on the right side of the *Quadrant*.

Who Pays The Most Taxes?

The rich pay few income taxes. Why? Simply because they do not earn their money as employees. The ultra rich know that the best way to avoid taxes legally is by generating that income out of the 'B' and 'I' quadrants.

If people earn money in the 'E' quadrant, the only tax break they are offered is to buy a bigger house and go into greater debt. From the right side of the *CASHFLOW Quadrant*, that is not too financially intelligent. To people on the right side, that is the same as saying, 'Give me $1, and I will give you $.50 back.'

72

Taxes Are Unfair

I often hear people say, 'It's un-American not to pay taxes.'

Americans who say this seem to have forgotten their history. America was founded out of tax protest. Have they forgotten the infamous Boston Tea Party of 1773? The rebellion that led to the Revolutionary War which separated the American colonies from the oppressive taxes of England.

This rebellion was followed by the Shay's Rebellion, The Whiskey Rebellion, Fries Rebellion, The Tariff Wars and many others throughout the history of the United States.

There are two other famous tax revolts that were not American, but also demonstrate the passion with which people object to taxation:

The story of William Tell is a story of tax protest. That is why the arrow was shot off his son's head. He was angry about taxes and risked his son's life in protest.

And then there was Lady Godiva. She asked that taxes in her town be lowered. The heads of the government said they would lower the taxes if she would ride naked through the town. She took them up on their dare.

Tax Advantages

73

Taxes are a necessity of modern civilization. Problems arise when taxes become abusive and mismanaged. In the next few years, millions of baby boomers will begin to retire. They will shift from the role of taxpayers to retirement and Social Security recipients. There will be a need to collect more taxes to support this shift. America and other great nations will decline financially. Individuals with money will leave in search of countries that welcome their money, instead of penalize them for having it.

A Big Mistake

Earlier this year, I was interviewed by a newspaper reporter. During the interview, he asked me how much money I made during the prior year. I replied, 'Approximately a million dollars.'

'And how much did you pay in taxes?' he asked.

'Nothing,' I said. 'That money was made in capital gains, and I was able to indefinitely defer paying those taxes. I sold three pieces of real estate and put them through a Tax Code Section 1031 exchange. I never touched the money. I just reinvested it into a much larger property.' A few days later, the newspaper ran this story.

'Rich man makes $1 million and admits to paying nothing in taxes.'

I did say something like that, but a few choice words are missing, thus distorting the message. I do not know if the reporter was being malicious or if he simply did not understand what a 1031 exchange was. Whatever the reason, it is a perfect example of different points of view coming from different quadrants. As I said, not all income is equal. Some income is much less taxed than others.

Most People Focus On Income Not Investments

The reporter earns his income in this column:

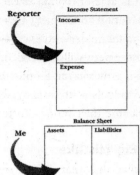

I earn my money in this column:

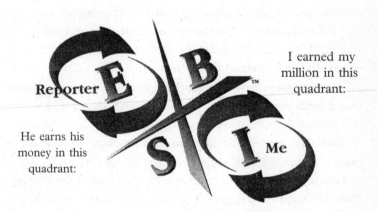

He earns his money in this quadrant:

Reporter

I earned my million in this quadrant:

Me

And today, I still hear people saying, 'I'm going back to school so I can get a raise,' or 'I'm working hard so I can get a promotion.'

Those are words or ideas of a person who is focusing on the income column of the financial statement or the 'E' quadrant of the *CASHFLOW Quadrant*. Those are the words of a person who will give half of that raise to the government and work harder and longer to do it.

In an upcoming chapter, I will explain how people on the right-hand side of the *Quadrant* utilize taxes as an asset, instead of the liability it is for most people on the left side of the *Quadrant*. It is not a matter of being unpatriotic; it's a matter of being a person who protests, and fights back legally, to defend the right to keep as much money as possible. People and countries that do not protest their taxes are often people or countries with depressed economies.

Get Rich Quickly

For my wife and me to go from homeless to financially free quickly meant earning our money in the 'B' and 'I' quadrants. In the right-hand quadrants, you can get rich quickly because you can avoid paying taxes legally. And by being able to keep more money and have that money work for us, we found freedom quickly.

How To Get Free

Taxes and debt are two of the main reasons most people never feel financially secure or achieve financial freedom. The path to security or freedom is found on the right-hand side of the *CASH-FLOW Quadrant*. You need to go beyond job security. It is time to know the difference between financial security and financial freedom.

What Is The Difference Between

1. JOB SECURITY,
2. FINANCIAL SECURITY, and
3. FINANCIAL FREEDOM?

As you know, my highly educated dad was fixated on job security, as are most people of his generation. He assumed that job security meant financial security . . . that was, until he lost his job

76

and could not get another job. My rich dad never talked about job security. He talked instead about financial freedom.

The answer to finding the kind of security or freedom you desire can be found in observing the patterns found in the *CASH-FLOW Quadrant.*

1. This Is The Pattern For Job Security

People with this pattern are often good at performing their job. Many spent years in school, and years on the job gaining experience. The problem is they know little about the 'B' quadrant or the 'I' quadrant, even if they have a retirement plan. They feel financially insecure because they have been trained only for job or professional security.

Two Legs Are Better Than One

To become more financially secure, I suggest, in addition to performing their jobs in the 'E' or 'S' quadrants, individuals become educated in the 'B' or 'I' quadrants. By having confidence in their abilities on both sides of the *Quadrant*, they will naturally feel more secure, even if they have only a little money. Knowledge is power . . . all they have to do is wait for the opportunity to use their knowledge and then they'll have the money.

That is why our maker gave us two legs. If we had only one leg, we would always feel wobbly and insecure. By having knowledge in two quadrants, one on the left and one on the right, we tend to feel more secure. People who know about their job or their profession only have one leg. Every time the economic winds blow, they tend to wobble more than people with two legs.

2. This Is The Pattern For Financial Security

This is what financial security looks like for an 'E':

Instead of just putting money into a retirement account and hoping for the best, this loop signifies that people feel confident in their education as both an investor and an employee. Just as we study at school to learn a job, I suggest you study to learn to be a professional investor.

The reporter who was upset about me making a million dollars in my asset column and not paying taxes never asked me the question, 'How did you make the million dollars?'

To me, that is the real question. Legally avoiding the taxes is easy. Making the million was not so easy.

A second path to financial security could be:

And this is what financial security looks like for an 'S':

This is the pattern described by the book *The Millionaire Next Door*, written by Thomas Stanley. It is an excellent book. The average American millionaire is self-employed, lives frugally, and invests for the long term. The pattern above reflects that financial life path.

This path, the 'S to the B,' is often the path that many great entrepreneurs, like Bill Gates, take. It is not the easiest, but in my mind, it is one of the best.

Two Is Better Than One

So being educated in more than one quadrant, especially one on the left and one on the right, is much better than being good in just one. In Chapter 2, I refer to the fact that the average rich person earns 70 percent from the right side and 30 percent from the left side of the *Quadrant*. I have found that no matter how much money people make, they will feel more secure if they operate in more than one quadrant. Financial security is having a secure footing on both sides of the *CASHFLOW Quadrant*.

Millionaire Firefighters

I have two friends who are examples of success on both sides of the *CASHFLOW Quadrant*. They have tremendous job security with benefits, and they have also achieved great financial wealth on the right side of the *Quadrant*. Both are firefighters working for the city government. They have good, steady pay, excellent benefits and retirement plans, and work only two days a week. Three days a week they work as professional investors. The remaining two days, they relax and spend with their families.

One buys old houses, fixes them up and collects rent. At the time of this writing, he owns 45 houses that pay him $10,000 a month net, after debt, taxes, maintenance, management and insurance. He earns $3,500 as a firefighter, making his total monthly income more than $13,000 and annual income about $150,000 and growing. He has five more years before retirement, and his goal is to have $200,000 a year in income at age 56. Not bad for a government employee with four kids.

The other friend spends his time analyzing companies and taking major long-term positions in stocks and options. His portfolio is now more than $3 million. If he cashed it out and earned 10 percent interest a year, he would have an income of $300,000 per year, barring any major market changes, for life. Again, not bad for a government employee with two kids.

Both friends have enough passive income from their 20 years of investing to have retired by age 40 . . . but they both enjoy their work and want to retire with full benefits from local government. They then will be free because they will enjoy the benefits of success from both sides of the *Quadrant*.

Money Alone Does Not Bring Security

I have met many people who have millions in their retirement accounts and still feel insecure. Why? Because it's money generated from their job or business. They often have the money invested in a retirement account, but know little to nothing about the subject of investments. If that money disappears, and their working days are over, what do they do then?

In times of great economic change, there are always great transfers of wealth. Even if you do not have much money, it is important to invest in your education . . . for when the changes come, you will be better prepared for them. Don't be caught unaware and afraid. As I said, no one can predict what will happen, yet it is best to be prepared for whatever happens. And that means getting educated now.

3. This Is The Pattern For Financial Freedom

This is the pattern of study my rich dad recommended. It is the path to financial freedom. This is true financial freedom because in the 'B' quadrant, people are working for you, and in the 'I' quadrant, your money is working for you. You are free to work or not to work. Your knowledge in these two quadrants has brought you complete physical freedom from work.

If you look at the ultra rich, this is their pattern in the *Quadrant*. The loop around the 'B' and the 'I' signifies the income pattern of Bill Gates of Microsoft, Rupert Murdoch of News Corp., Warren Buffet of Berkshire Hathaway, and Ross Perot.

A quick word of caution. The 'B' quadrant is much different from the 'I' quadrant. I have seen many successful 'B's' sell their businesses for millions, and their new-found wealth goes to their head. They tend to think that their dollars are a measure of their IQ, so they swagger on down to the 'I' quadrant and lose it all. The game and rules are different in all of the quadrants . . . which is why I recommend education over ego.

Just as in the case of financial security, having two quadrants gives you greater stability in the world of financial freedom.

A Choice Of Paths

These are the different financial paths people can choose. Unfortunately, most people choose the path of job security. When the economy starts wobbling, they often cling more desperately to job security. They wind up spending their lives there.

At a minimum, I recommend becoming educated in financial security, which is feeling confident about your job and feeling confident about your ability to invest in good times and in bad times. A big secret is that true investors make more money in bad markets. They make their money because the non-investors are panicking and selling when they should be buying. That is why I am not afraid of the possible coming economic changes . . . because change means wealth is being transferred.

Your Boss Cannot Make You Rich

The economic changes currently happening are partly from the sales and mergers of companies. Recently, a friend of mine sold his company. He put more than $15 million into his bank account the day of the sale. His employees had to look for new jobs.

At the farewell party, which was filled with tears, there were also undercurrents of extreme anger and resentment. Although he had paid them well for years, most workers were no financially better off on their last day of work than they were on their first day of work. Many people realized that the owner of the company had gotten rich while they spent all those years collecting their paychecks and paying bills.

The reality is, your boss's job is not to make you rich. Your boss's job is to make sure you get your paycheck. It is your job to become rich, if you want to. And that job begins the moment you receive your paycheck. If you have poor money-management skills, then all the money in the world cannot save you. If you budget your money wisely, and learn about either the 'B' or 'I' quadrant, then you are on your own path to great personal fortune and, most importantly, freedom.

My rich dad used to say to his son and me, 'The only difference between a rich person and a poor person is what they do in their spare time.'

I agree with that statement. I realize that people are busier than ever before, and free time is more and more precious. Yet, I would like to suggest that if you are going to be busy anyway, be busy on both sides of the *Quadrant*. If you do that, you will have a better chance of eventually finding more free time and more financial freedom. When at work, work hard. Please do not read the 'Wall Street Journal' on company time. Your boss will appreciate and respect you more. What you do after work with your paycheck and your spare time will determine your future. If you work hard on the left side of the *Quadrant*, you will work hard forever. If you work hard on the right side of the *Quadrant*, you have a chance of finding freedom.

The Path I Recommend

I am often asked by people on the left side of the *Quadrant*, 'What would you recommend?' I recommend the same path my rich dad recommended to me. The same path that people like Ross Perot, Bill Gates and others took. The path looks like this:

I occasionally receive this complaint, 'But I'd rather be an investor.'

To which I reply, 'Then go to the 'I' quadrant. If you have plenty of money and lots of free time, go straight to the 'I' quadrant. But if you don't have an abundance of time and money, the path I recommend is safer.'

In most cases, people do not have an abundance of time or money, so they then ask another question, 'Why? Why do you recommend the 'B' quadrant first?'

This discussion usually takes an hour or so, which I will not go into here. But I will summarize my reasons in the next few lines.

1. **Experience and education.** If you are first successful as a 'B,' you will have a better chance of developing into a powerful 'I.'

'I's' invest in 'B's'

If you first develop a solid business sense, you can become a better investor. You will be better able to identify other good 'B's.' True investors invest in successful 'B's' with stable business systems. It is risky to invest in an 'E' or an 'S' who does not know the difference between a system and a product . . . or who lacks excellent leadership skills.

2. **Cash Flow.** If you have a business that is up and running, you then should have the free time and the cash flow to support the ups and downs of the 'I' quadrant.

Many times I meet people from the 'E–S' quadrants who are so tight on cash, they could not afford to take any kind of financial loss. One market swing and they are wiped out financially because they operate financially at 'red line.'

The reality is, investing is capital and knowledge intensive. Sometimes it takes lots of capital and time to gain that knowledge. Many successful investors have lost many times before winning. Successful people know that success is a poor teacher. Learning comes from making mistakes, and in the 'I' quadrant, mistakes cost money. If you lack both knowledge and capital, it's financial suicide to try to become an investor.

By developing the skill of becoming a good 'B' first, you will also be providing the cash flow necessary to move on to becoming a good investor. The business you develop as a 'B' will provide the cash to support you as you gain the education to become a good investor. Once you have gained the education to become a successful investor you will understand how I can say 'It does not always take money to make money.'

Good News

The good news is that it is now easier than ever before to be successful in the 'B' quadrant. Just as there have been technological advances that have made many things easier, technology also has made it easier to be successful in the 'B' quadrant. Although it's not as easy as just getting a minimum-wage job, the systems are in place now for more and more people to find financial success as 'B's.'

CHAPTER FOUR

The 3 Kinds Of Business Systems

In moving to the 'B' quadrant, remember that your goal is to own a system and have people work that system for you. You can develop the business system yourself or you can look for a system to purchase. Think of the system as the bridge that will allow you to cross safely from the left side of the *CASHFLOW Quadrant* to the right side . . . your bridge to financial freedom.

There are three main types of business systems commonly in use today. They are:

1. Traditional C-type corporations – where you develop your own system.
2. Franchises – where you buy an existing system.
3. Network Marketing – where you buy into and become part of an existing system.

Each has its strengths and weaknesses, yet each ultimately does the same thing. If operated properly, each system will provide a steady stream of income without much physical effort on the part of the owner . . . once it is up and running. The problem is getting it up and running.

In 1985, when people asked, 'Why were you homeless?' Kim and I simply said, 'We were building a business system.'

It was a business system that was a hybrid of the traditional C-type corporation and a franchise. As stated before, the 'B' quadrant requires a knowledge of both systems and people.

Our decision to develop our own system meant a lot of hard work. I had taken this route before, and my company had failed. Although it was successful for years, it suddenly went broke in its fifth year. When success came to us, we were not ready with an adequate system. The system began to break down even though we had hard-working people. We felt like we were on a good-size yacht that had sprung a leak, but we could not find the leak. All of us were trying to figure out where the leak was, but we could not bail water fast enough to find the leak and fix it. Even if we found it, we were not certain we could plug it.

'You May Lose 2 Or 3 Companies'

When I was in high school, my rich dad told his son and me that he had lost a company when he was in his 20s. 'That was the best and worst experience of my life,' he said. 'As much as I hated it, I learned more by repairing it and eventually turning it into a huge success.'

Knowing that I was contemplating starting my own company, rich dad said to me, 'You may lose two or three companies, before you build a successful one that lasts.'

He was training Mike, his son, to take over his empire. Because my dad was a government employee, I was not going to inherit an empire. I had to build my own.

Success Is A Poor Teacher

'Success is a poor teacher,' rich dad always said. 'We learn the most about ourselves when we fail . . . so don't be afraid of failing. Failing is part of the process of success. You cannot have success without failure. So unsuccessful people are people who never fail.'

Maybe it was a self-fulfilling prophecy, but in 1984, the company that went down was company No. 3. I had made millions and had lost millions and was starting all over again when I met Kim. The reason I know she did not marry me for my money is because I did not have any money. When I told her what I was going to do, build company No. 4, she did not back away.

'I'll build it with you,' was her reply, and she was true to her word. Along with another partner, we built a business system with 11 offices worldwide that generated income regardless of whether we worked. Building it from nothing to 11 offices took five years of blood, sweat and tears . . . but it worked. Both dads were happy for me and sincerely congratulated me (they had both lost money in my previous experiments at starting companies).

The Hard Part

Mike, my rich dad's son, has often said to me, 'I will never know if I can do what you did or my dad did. The system was handed to me, and all I had to do was learn how to run it.'

I am certain he could have developed his own successful system because he learned well from his dad. Yet, I understand what he meant. The hard thing about building a company from scratch is that you have two big variables: the system and the people building the system. If both the people and the system are leaky, the chances for failure are great. Sometimes it is hard to know whether the problem is the person or the system that is failing.

Before Franchises

When my rich dad began teaching me about becoming a 'B,' there was only one kind of business. That was big business . . . a major corporation that usually dominated the town. In our town in Hawaii, it was the sugar plantation that controlled virtually everything . . . including the other big businesses. So there were big businesses and mom-and-pop 'S'-type businesses with little in between.

To be able to work at the top levels of those big sugar companies was not a likely goal for people like rich dad and me. Minorities, such as the Japanese, Chinese and Hawaiians worked in the fields, but were never allowed in the boardroom. So rich dad learned everything he knew simply by trial and error.

As I started high school, we began to hear about a thing called 'franchises,' but none had come to our little town. We had not heard about McDonald's or Kentucky Fried Chicken or Taco Bell. They were not a part of our vocabulary while I was studying with rich dad. When we did hear rumors about them, we heard they were 'illegal, fraudulent scams and dangerous.' Naturally, upon hearing those rumors, rich dad flew to California to begin checking franchises out, rather than believing the gossip. When he returned, all he said was, 'Franchises are the wave of the future,' and he bought the rights to two of them. His wealth skyrocketed as the idea of franchises caught on, and he began selling his rights to other people so they could have a chance at building their own businesses.

When I asked him if I should buy one from him, he simply said, 'No. You've come this far in learning how to build your own business system; don't stop now. Franchises are for people who do not want to build or do not know how to build their own systems. Besides, you don't have the $250,000 it takes to buy a franchise from me.'

It is hard to imagine today a city without a McDonald's or Burger King or Pizza Hut on every corner. Yet, there was a time, not too long ago, when they did not exist. And I'm old enough to remember those days.

How To Learn To Become A 'B'

The way I learned to become a 'B' was by being an apprentice to my rich dad. His son and I were both 'E's' learning to be 'B's.' And that is the way many people learn. It's called 'on-the-job training.' This is the way many closely held family empires are passed on from one generation to the next.

The problem is, not too many people are privileged or lucky enough to learn the 'behind-the-scene' aspects of becoming a 'B.' Most corporate 'management-training programs' are just that – the company only trains you to be a manager. Few teach what it takes to be a 'B.'

Often people get stuck in the 'S' quadrant in their journey to the 'B' quadrant. This happens primarily because they do not develop a strong enough system, and so they end up becoming an integral part of the system. Successful 'B's' develop a system that will run without their involvement.

There are three ways you can make it to the 'B' side quickly.

1. **Find a mentor.** My rich dad was my mentor. A mentor is someone who has already done what you want to do . . . and is successful at doing it. Do not find an adviser. An adviser is someone who tells you how to do it, but has not personally done it. Most advisers are in the 'S' quadrant. The world is filled with 'S's' trying to tell you how to be

a 'B' or an 'I.' My rich dad was a mentor, not an adviser.

One of the biggest tips my rich dad gave me was this:

'Be careful of the advice you take. While you must keep your mind open, always be first aware of which quadrant the advice is coming from.'

My rich dad taught me about systems and how to be a leader of people, not a manager of people. Managers often see their subordinates as inferiors. Leaders must direct people who are often smarter.

If you would like to read an excellent book about the basics of starting your own business system, check out *E-Myth*, by Michael Gerber. For people who want to learn to develop their own system, this book is priceless.

A traditional way of learning about systems is to get your MBA from a prestigious school and get a fast-track job up the corporate ladder. An MBA is important because you learn the basics of accounting and how the financial numbers relate to the systems of a business. Yet, just because you have an MBA does not automatically mean you are competent to run all the systems that ultimately make up a complete business system.

To learn about all the systems necessary in a big company, you'll need to spend 10 to 15 years there, learning all the different aspects of the business. You should then be prepared to leave and start your own company. Working for a successful major corporation is like being paid by your mentor.

Even with a mentor and/or years of experience, this first method is labor intensive. To create your own system requires a lot of trial and error, up-front legal costs, and paperwork. All of this occurs at the same time you are trying to develop your people.

2. **Franchises.** Another way to learn about systems is to buy a franchise. When you buy a franchise, you are buying a

'tried and proven' operating system. There are many excellent franchises.

By buying the franchise system, instead of trying to create your own, you can focus on developing your people. Buying the system removes one big variable when you are learning how to be a 'B.' The reason many banks will loan money on a franchise and not to a small start-up business is because the banks recognize the importance of systems and how starting with a good system will lower their risk.

A word of caution if you buy a franchise. Please do not be an 'S' who wants to 'do their own thing.' If you buy a franchise system, be an 'E.' Just do it exactly the way they tell you to do it. Nothing is more tragic than the courtroom fights between franchisees and franchisors. The fights occur usually because the people who buy the system really want to do it their way, not the way the person who created the system wants it run. If you want to do your own thing, then do it after you've mastered both systems and people.

My highly educated dad failed even though he bought a famous and expensive ice-cream franchise. Although the system was excellent, the business still failed. In my opinion, the franchise failed because the people he was in partnership with were all 'E's' and 'S's' who did not know what to do when things started to get bad, and did not ask for support from the parent company. In the end, the partners fought among themselves, and the business went down. They forgot that a true 'B' is more than a system. It is also dependent on good people to operate the system.

Banks Don't Lend Money To People Without Systems

If a bank will not lend money to a small business without a system, why should you? Almost daily, people come to me with business plans with the hope of raising money for their idea or their project.

93

Most of the time I turn them down for one main reason. The people raising the money do not know the difference between a product and a system. I have had friends (singers in a band) ask me to invest money in developing a new music CD, and others who want me to help form a new nonprofit to change the world. As much as I might like the project, the product or the person, I will turn them down if they have little or no experience in creating and running business systems.

Just because you can sing does not mean you understand the system of marketing, or the system of finance and accounting, and the system of sales, and the system of hiring and firing people, and the legal system, and the many other systems that are required to keep a business afloat and make it successful.

For a business to survive and thrive, 100 percent of all the systems must be functioning and accountable. For example:

An airplane is a system of systems. If an airplane takes off and, let's say, the fuel system fails, there often is a crash. The same things happen in business. It's not the systems that you know about that are the problem – it's the systems you are not aware of that cause you to crash.

The human body is a system of systems. Most of us have had a loved one die because one of the body systems has failed – like the blood system, which causes disease to spread to all of the other systems.

That is why building a tried-and-true business system is not easy. It is the systems you forget about or do not pay attention to that cause you to crash and burn. That is why I rarely invest with an 'E' or 'S' who has a new product or idea. Professional investors tend to invest in proven systems with people who know how to run those systems.

So if banks lend based only on tried-and-true systems, and look to the person who is going to run them, then you should do the same – if you want to be a smart investor.

3. **Network marketing.** Also called multilevel marketing or direct distribution systems. Just as with franchises, the legal system initially attempted to outlaw network marketing, and I know of some countries that have succeeded in outlawing or severely restricting it. Any new system or idea often goes through this period of being classified as 'strange and suspicious.' At first, I also thought that network marketing was a scam. But over the years, I have studied the various systems available through network marketing, and I have watched several friends become successful at this form of 'B.' I have changed my mind.

After I dropped my prejudices and began researching network marketing, I found that there were many people who were sincerely and diligently building successful network marketing businesses. When I met these people, I saw the impact their business had on other people's lives and financial futures. I began to truly appreciate the value of the network marketing system. For a reasonable entry fee (often around $200), people can buy into an existing system and immediately start building their business. Due to the technological advances in the computer industry, these organizations are totally automated, and the headaches of paperwork, order processing, distribution, accounting and follow-up are almost entirely managed by the network marketing software systems. New distributors can focus all of their efforts in building their business through sharing this automated business opportunity instead of worrying about the normal start-up headaches of a small business.

One of my old friends who did more than a billion dollars in real estate in 1997 recently signed on as a network marketing distributor and began building his business. I was surprised to find him so diligently building a network marketing business because he definitely did not need the money. When I asked him why, he explained it this way:

'I went to school to become a CPA, and I have an MBA in finance. When people ask me how I became so rich, I tell them about the multimillion-dollar real estate transactions I do and the hundreds of thousands of dollars in passive income I receive each year from my real estate. I then notice that some of them withdraw or shy away. We both know that their chances of doing multimillion-dollar real estate investments like I do are slim to none. Besides not having the educational background, they do not have the extra capital to invest. So I began to look for a way I could help them achieve the same level of passive income I developed from real estate . . . without going back to school for six years and spending 12 years investing in real estate. I believe network marketing gives people the opportunity to build up the passive income they need for support while they learn to become professional investors. That is why I recommend network marketing to them. Even if they have little money, they can still invest "sweat equity" for five years and begin to generate more than enough passive income to begin investing. By developing their own business, they have the free time to learn and the capital to invest with me in my bigger deals.'

My friend joined a network marketing company as a distributor, after researching several, and started a network marketing business with people who someday want to invest with him. He is now doing well in his network marketing business as well as in his investment business. He told me, 'I did it initially because I wanted to help people find the money to invest, and now I'm getting rich from a whole new business.'

Twice a month, he holds classes on Saturdays. At the first meeting, he teaches people about business systems and people, or how to develop into a successful 'B.' On the second meeting of the month, he teaches them about financial literacy and financial intelligence. He is teaching them to be savvy 'I's.' His class sizes are growing rapidly.

The pattern he recommends is the same one I recommend.

A Personal Franchise

And that's why today I recommend people consider network marketing. Many famous franchises cost a million dollars or more to buy. Network marketing is like buying a personal franchise, often for less than $200.

I know much of network marketing is hard work. But success in any quadrant is hard work. I personally generate no income as a network marketing distributor. I have researched several network marketing companies and their compensation plans. While doing my research, I did join several companies, just because their products were so good and I use them as a consumer.

Yet, if I could give you a recommendation as to finding a good organization to help you get over to the right side of the *Quadrant*, the key is not so much the product but the education the organization offers. There are network marketing organizations that are only interested in having you sell their system to your friends. And there are organizations primarily interested in educating you and helping you succeed.

From my research into network marketing, I have found two

important things you can learn through their programs that are essential in becoming a successful 'B':

1. To be successful, you need to learn to overcome your fear of being rejected, and to stop worrying about what other people will say about you. So many times I have met people who hold themselves back simply because of what their friends might say if they did something different. I know because I was the same way. Coming from a small town, everyone knew what everyone else was up to. If someone did not like what you were doing, the whole town heard about it and made your business their business.

One of the best phrases I said over and over to myself was, 'What you think of me is none of my business. What is most important is what I think about myself.'

One of the reasons my rich dad encouraged me to work in sales for Xerox Corporation for four years was not because he liked copiers, but because he wanted me to overcome my shyness and fear of rejection.

2. To learn to lead people. Working with different kinds of people is the hardest thing about business. The people I have met who are successful in any business are those who are natural leaders. The ability to get along with and inspire people is a priceless skill. A skill that can be learned.

As I said, the transition from the left quadrant to the right quadrant is not so much what you do, but who you have to become. Learn how to handle rejection, how not to be affected by what other people think of you, and learn to lead people and you will find prosperity. So I endorse any network marketing organization that is first committed to developing you as a human being, more than developing you into a salesperson. I would seek organizations that:

1. Are proven organizations that have successful track records and a distribution system and a compensation plan that has been successful for years.
2. Have a business opportunity you can succeed with, believe in and share confidently with others.
3. Have ongoing, long-term educational programs to develop you as a human being. Self-confidence is vital on the right side of the *Quadrant*.
4. Have a strong mentor program. You want to learn from leaders, not advisers. People who are already leaders on the right side of the *Quadrant* and want you to succeed.
5. Have people you respect and enjoy being with.

If the organization meets these five criteria, then and only then look at the product. Too many people look at the product and not the business system and organization behind the product. In some of the organizations I have looked into, one of their pitches was, 'The product sells itself. It's easy.' If you're looking to be a salesperson, an 'S,' then the product is the most important thing. But if you're developing into a long term 'B,' then the system, lifelong education, and the people are more important.

A friend and colleague of mine knowledgeable in this industry reminded me about the value of time, one of our most precious assets. A true success story in a network marketing company is when your commitment of time and hard work in the short term results in significant long-term passive income. Once you have built a strong organization below you, you can stop working and your revenue stream will continue from the efforts of the organization you have built. The most important key to success with a network marketing company is still, however, a long-term commitment on your part, as well as the organization's part, to mold you into the business leader you want to become.

A System Is A Bridge To Freedom

Being homeless was not an experience I want to repeat. Yet, for Kim and me, the experience was priceless. Today, freedom and security are found not so much in what we have, but what we know we can create with confidence.

Since that time we have created or helped develop a real estate company, an oil company, a mining company, and two education companies. So the process of learning how to create a successful system was beneficial for us. Yet, I would not recommend the process to anyone, unless they truly want to go through it.

Until only a few years ago, the possibility of a person becoming successful in the 'B' quadrant was only available to those who were brave or rich. Kim and I must have been brave because we certainly weren't rich. The reason so many people stay stuck in the left side of the *Quadrant* is because they feel the risks involved in developing their own system are too great. For them, it is smarter to remain safe and secure in a job.

Today, primarily due to changes in technology, the risk in becoming a successful business owner has been greatly reduced . . . and the opportunity to own your own business system has been made available to virtually everyone.

Franchises and network marketing took away the hard part of developing your own system. You acquire the rights to a proven system, and then your only job is to develop your people.

Think of these business systems as bridges. Bridges that will provide a path for you to cross safely from the left side to the right side of the *CASHFLOW Quadrant* . . . your bridge to financial freedom.

In the next chapter, I will cover the second half of the right side of the *Quadrant*, the 'I,' or investor.

CHAPTER FIVE
The 7 Levels Of Investors

My rich dad once asked me, 'What is the difference between a person who bets on horses and a person who picks stocks?'

'I don't know,' was my response.

'Not much,' was his answer, 'Never be the person who buys the stock. What you want to be when you grow up is the person who creates the stock that brokers sell and others buy.'

For a long time, I did not understand what my rich dad really meant. It was not until I started teaching investing to others that I really understood the different types of investors.

A special thanks goes to John Burley for this chapter. John is considered one of the brightest minds in the world of real estate investing. In his late 20s and early 30s, he purchased more than 130 homes using none of his own money. By the time he was 32, he was financially free and never had to work again. So, like me, he chooses to teach. But his knowledge goes far beyond just real estate. He began his career as a financial planner, so he has a deep understanding of the world of finance and taxes. But he also has the unique ability to explain it clearly. He has the gift of taking the complex or abstract and making it simple to understand. Through his teaching, he developed a way to identify investors into six categories by their level of sophistication in their investing as well as their differences in personality traits. I have revised and expanded his categories to include a seventh.

Using this identification method in concert with the *CASH-FLOW Quadrant* has helped me teach others about the world of investors. As you read about the different levels, you will probably recognize people you know at each level.

Optional Learning Exercise

At the end of each level, I have left a blank space where you can fill in the person or persons who, in your judgment, fit this level. When you find the level you are at, you may want to put your own name there.

As I said, this is only an optional exercise for the purpose of increasing your understanding of the different levels. It is in no way meant to degrade or put down your friends. The subject of money is as volatile as politics, religion and sex. That is why I recommend keeping your personal thoughts private. The blank space at the end of every level is merely there to enhance your learning, if you choose to use it.

I use this list often at the beginning of my investment classes. It has made the learning more powerful and has helped many students become clear on which level they are on and which level they want to go to.

Over the years, I have, with John's permission, modified the content to match my own experiences. Please read the seven levels carefully.

The Seven Levels Of Investors

Level 0: Those With Nothing To Invest

These people have no money to invest. They either spend everything they make or spend more than they make. There are many 'rich' people who would fall into this category because they spend as much, or more, than they make. Unfortunately this zero level is where about 50 percent of the adult population would be categorized.

Do you know any Level 0 investors? (optional)

_____

_____

Level 1: Borrowers

These people solve financial problems by borrowing money. Often they even invest with borrowed money. Their idea of financial planning is robbing Peter to pay Paul. They live their financial lives with their heads in the sand like ostriches, hoping and praying that everything will work out. While they may have a few assets, the reality is that their level of debt is simply too high. For the most part, they are not conscious about money and their spending habits.

Anything they own of value has debt attached to it. They use credit cards impulsively and then roll that debt into a long-term home-equity loan so they can clean up their credit cards and then start charging again. If the value of their home goes up, they borrow on the equity again, or buy a larger and more expensive home. They believe the value of real estate only goes up.

The words 'low down, easy monthly payments' always draw their attention. They often purchase depreciating toys (or doodads) such as boats, swimming pools, vacations and cars with those words in mind. They list these depreciating toys as assets and go back to the bank for another loan and wonder why they get turned down.

Shopping is their favorite form of exercise. They buy things they don't need, saying these words to themselves: 'Oh, go ahead. You deserve it.' Or 'You're worth it.' Or 'If I don't buy it now, I may never find it again at such a great price.' Or 'It's on sale.' Or 'I want the kids to have what I never had.'

They think spreading debt over a long period of time is smart, always kidding themselves that they'll work harder and pay off their bills someday. They spend everything they make and then some. They are known as consumers. Shop owners and car dealers love these people. If they have money, it gets spent. If they don't have the money, they borrow it.

When asked what their problem is, they will say that they just don't make enough money. They think more money will solve the problem. No matter how much they make, they only get deeper into debt. Little do most of them realize that the money they earn today seemed like a fortune or dream to them just yesterday. But today, even though they have achieved their dream income, it still is not enough.

They fail to see that the problem is not necessarily their income (or lack of it), but rather their money habits. Some eventually believe deep down that their situation is hopeless and have given up. So they bury their head deeper and keep on doing the same things. Their habits of borrowing, shopping and spending are out of control. Just as a binge eater eats when depressed, these people spend when depressed. They spend, get depressed and spend more.

They often argue with loved ones about money, emphatically defending their need to buy this or that. They live in complete financial denial, pretending that miraculously their money problems will someday disappear, or they pretend they will always have enough money to spend on whatever they desire.

This level of investor can often look rich. They may have big houses and flashy cars . . . but if you check, they buy on borrowed money. They may also make a lot of money, but they are one professional accident away from financial ruin.

I had an ex-business owner in one of my classes. He was well known in the 'make big bucks, spend big bucks' category. He had a thriving chain of jewelry stores for years. But one downturn in the economy and his business disappeared. His debts, however, did not go away. It took less than six months for those debts to eat him alive. He was in my class looking for new answers and refused to even entertain the idea that he and his wife were Level 1 investors.

He came from the 'B' quadrant, hoping to get rich in the 'I' quadrant. He clung to the idea that he was once a successful businessman and could use the same formulas to invest his way to financial freedom. It was a classic case of a businessman thinking he could automatically become a successful investor. The rules of business are not always the same as the rules of investing.

Unless these investors are willing to change, their financial future is bleak . . . unless they marry someone rich who will put up with such habits.

Do you know any Level 1 investors? (optional)

_____

_____

Level 2: Savers
These people put aside a 'small' amount of money (usually) on a regular basis. The money is in a low-risk, low-return vehicle such as a money-market checking account, savings account or certificate of deposit (CD).

If they have an Individual Retirement Account (IRA), they have it with a bank or in a mutual-fund cash account.

They often save to consume rather than to invest (e.g. they save for a new TV, car, vacation, etc.). They believe in paying in cash. They are afraid of credit and debt. Instead, they like the 'security' of money in the bank.

Even when shown that in today's economic environment

savings give a negative return (after inflation and taxes), they are still unwilling to take on much risk. Little do they know that the U.S. dollar has lost 90 percent of its value since 1950, and continues to lose value annually at a rate greater than the interest a bank pays them. They often have whole-life insurance policies because they love the feeling of security.

People in this group often waste their most precious asset, which is time, trying to save pennies. They spend hours clipping coupons from the newspaper, and then at the supermarket, they hold up everyone else in line, fumbling to find those big savings.

Instead of trying to save pennies, they could have put that time into learning how to invest. If they had put $10,000 into John Templeton's fund in 1954 and forgotten about it, it would have been worth $2.4 million in 1994. Or if they had put $10,000 into George Soros' Quantum Fund in 1969, it would have been worth $22.1 million in 1994. Instead, their deep need for security, which is fear-based, keeps them saving in low-yield investments, such as bank CD's.

You often hear these people saying, 'A penny saved is a penny earned.' Or 'I'm saving for the kids.' The real truth is there is often some deep insecurity running them and their lives. In truth, they often 'shortchange' themselves and the people they are saving for. They are almost the exact opposite of the Level 1 investor.

Saving money was a good idea during the Agrarian Age. But once we entered the Industrial Age, savings was not the smart choice. Simply saving money became an even worse choice once the U.S. went off the gold standard and we hit the era of inflation with government rampantly printing money. People who save money during times of inflation end up as losers. Of course, if we go into a period of deflation, they may be winners . . . but only if the printed money is still worth something.

It is good to have some savings. It is recommended that you have six months' to a year's worth of living expenses held in cash.

But after that, there are far better and safer investment vehicles than money in the bank. To hold your money in the bank earning 5 percent while others are getting 15 percent and more is not a wise investment strategy.

Yet, if you are unwilling to study investing and you live in constant fear of financial risk, then saving is a better choice than investing. You don't have to think as much if you just keep the money in the bank . . . and your bankers will love you. Why shouldn't they? The bank lends $10 to $20 for every $1 you have in savings and charges up to 19 percent interest, then turns around and pays you less than 5 percent. We should all be bankers.

Do you know any Level 2 investors? (optional)

_____

_____

Level 3: 'Smart' Investors
There are three different types of investors in this group. This level of investor is aware of the need to invest. They may even participate in the company retirement plan 401(k), SEP, Superannuation, pension, etc. Sometimes they even have outside investments in mutual funds, stocks, bonds or limited partnerships.

Generally they are intelligent people who have a solid education. They make up the two-thirds of the country we call the 'middle class.' However, when it comes to investing, they are often not educated . . . or lack what the investment industry calls 'sophistication.' Rarely will they read a company annual report or company prospectus. How could they? They were not trained to read financial reports. They lack financial literacy. They may have advanced college degrees, and may be doctors or even accountants, but few have ever been formally trained and educated in the win/lose world of investing.

These are the three main categories in this level. They are often smart people who are well educated and often make substantial incomes, and they do invest. Yet, there are differences.

Level 3-A. People in this level make up the 'I Can't Be Bothered' group. They have convinced themselves they don't understand money and never will. They say things like,

'I'm just not very good with numbers.'

'I'll never understand how investing works.'

'I'm just too busy.'

'There's too much paperwork.'

'It's just too complicated.'

'Investing is too risky.'

'I prefer to leave the money decisions to the professionals.'

'It's too much of a hassle.'

'My husband/wife handles the investments for our family.'

These people just let the money sit and do little in their retirement plan or turn it over to a financial planner who recommends 'diversification.' They block their financial future out of their minds, work hard day to day, and say to themselves, 'At least I have a retirement plan.'

When they retire, then they'll look at how their investments did.

Do you know any Level 3-A investors? (optional)

_____

_____

Level 3-B. The second category is the 'Cynic.' These people know all the reasons why an investment will not work. They are dangerous to have around. They often sound intelligent, speak with authority, are successful in their chosen field, but are really cowards under their intellectual exterior. They can tell you exactly how and why you will get 'swindled' with every investment known to man. When you ask for their opinion on a stock or other investment, you walk away feeling terrible, often afraid or doubtful. Their most commonly repeated words are, 'Well, I've been taken before. They're not going to do that to me again.'

They often drop names and say things like, 'My broker at Merrill Lynch, or Dean Witter . . .' Name dropping helps cover their deep insecurity.

Yet strangely, these same cynics often follow the market like sheep. At work, they're always reading the financial pages or the 'Wall Street Journal'. They read the paper and then tell everyone else what they know at the coffee break. Their language is filled with the latest investment jargon and technical terms. They talk about the big deals, but are never in them. They look for stocks that make the front page and, if the report is favorable, they often buy. The problem is they buy late because if you get your news from the newspaper . . . it is too late. The truly smart investors have bought way before it makes the news. The cynic does not know that.

When bad news comes, they criticize and say things like, 'I knew it.' They think they're in the game, but they are really only a spectator standing on the sidelines. They often want to get into the game, but deep down they are terribly afraid of getting hurt. Security is more important than fun.

Psychiatrists report that cynicism is the combination of fear and ignorance, which in turn causes arrogance. These people often enter major market swings late, waiting for the crowd or social proof that their investment decision is the right decision. Because they wait for social proof, they buy late at market tops and sell at market bottoms, just as the market crashes. They label buying high and selling low as getting 'swindled' again. Everything they were so afraid of happening . . . happens, again and again.

Cynics are often what professional traders call 'pigs.' They squeal a lot and then run to their own slaughter. They buy high and sell low. Why? Because they're so 'smart', they have become overly cautious. They are smart, but are terrified of taking risks and making mistakes, so they study harder, get smarter. The more they know, the more risk they see, so they study even harder. Their cynical caution causes them to wait until it's too late. They come to market when greed finally overpowers their fear. They come to the trough with the other pigs and get slaughtered.

But the worst part of the cynic is that they infect the people around them with their deep fear, disguised as intelligence. When it comes to investing, they can tell you why things won't work, but they can't tell you how it could work. The worlds of academia, government, religion and the media are filled with these people. They love hearing about financial disaster or wrongdoings so they can 'spread the word.' They are truly 'Monday-morning quarterbacks' when it comes to investing. Yet, rarely do they have anything good to say about financial success. A cynic finds it easy to discover what is wrong. It is their way of protecting themselves from revealing their lack of knowledge – or lack of courage.

The original Cynics were an ancient Greek sect despised because of their arrogance and sarcastic contempt for merit and success. They were nicknamed the dog-men (cynic comes from the Greek word for dog). When it comes to money, there are many dog-people . . . many who are smart, and well-educated. Be careful about allowing dog-people to squelch your financial dreams. While it is true that the world of money is filled with crooks, con-men and charlatans, what industry isn't?

It is possible to get rich quickly, with little money, and with little risk. It is possible, but only if you are willing to do your part to make it possible. One of the things you need to do is keep an open mind and be aware of cynics as well as con-men. They are both financially dangerous.

Do you know any Level 3-B investors? (optional)

_____

_____

Level 3-C. The third category of this level is the 'Gambler.' This group is also called 'pigs' by professional traders. But while the 'cynic' is overly cautious, this group is not cautious enough. They look at the stock market, or any investment market, about the same way they look at a Las Vegas craps table. It's just luck. Throw the dice and pray.

This group has not set trading rules or principles. They want to act like the 'Big Boys,' so they fake it until they make it or lose it all. The latter is most probable. They are searching for the 'secret' to investing, or the 'Holy Grail.' They are always looking for new and exciting ways to invest. Instead of long-term diligence and study and understanding, they seek 'tips' or 'shortcuts.'

They jump into commodities, initial public offerings (IPOs), penny stocks, gas and oil, cattle and every other investment known to mankind. They like to use 'sophisticated' investment techniques such as margins, puts, calls and options. They jump into the 'game' without knowing who the players are and who makes up the rules.

These people are the worst investors the planet has ever known. They always try to hit a 'home run.' They usually 'strike out.' When asked how they are doing, they always are 'about even,' or 'a little bit up.' In actuality, they have lost money. Lots of money. Often huge amounts of money. This type of investor loses money over 90 percent of the time. They never discuss their losses. They only remember the 'killing' they made six years ago. They think they were smart and fail to recognize they were merely lucky. They think that all they need is 'the one big deal' and then they'll be on easy street. Society calls this person an 'incurable gambler.' Deep down, they are simply lazy when it comes to investing money.

Do you know any Level 3-C investors? (optional)

_____

_____

Level 4: Long-term Investors

These investors are clearly aware of the need to invest. They are actively involved in their own investment decisions. They have a clearly laid out long-term plan that will allow them to reach their financial objectives. They invest in their education before actually buying an investment. They take advantage of periodic investing and, whenever possible, invest in a tax-advantaged way. Most importantly they seek out advice from competent financial planners.

Please understand this type of investor is not what you would think of as some big-time investor. Far from it. It is doubtful that they are investing in real estate, businesses, commodities, or any other exciting investment vehicles. Rather, they take the conservative long-term approach recommended by investors such as Peter Lynch of Fidelity's Magellan Fund fame, or Warren Buffett.

If you are not yet a long-term investor, get yourself there as fast as you can. What does this mean? This means that you sit down and map out a plan. Get control of your spending habits. Minimize your debt and liabilities. Live within your means and then increase your means. Find out how much invested per month for how many months at a realistic rate of return it will take to reach your goals. Goals such as: At what age do you plan to stop working? How much money will you need per month?

Simply having a long-term plan that reduces your consumer debt while putting away a small amount of money (on a periodic basis) into a top mutual fund will give you a head start on retiring wealthy, if you start early enough and keep an eye on what you're doing.

At this level, keep it simple. Don't get fancy. Forget the sophisticated investments. Just do solid stock and mutual fund investments. Learn how to buy closed-end mutual funds soon, if you haven't already. Don't try to outsmart the market. Use insurance vehicles wisely as protection but not as wealth accumulation. A mutual fund like the Vanguard Index 500 fund, which in the past has outperformed two-thirds of all mutual funds year-in and year-out is worth using as a benchmark. Over 10 years, this type of fund may give you a return that exceeds 90 percent of the 'professional' mutual-fund money managers. But always remember, there is no '100 percent safe investment.' Index funds have their own inherent tragic flaws.

Stop waiting for the 'big deal.' Get into the 'game' with small deals (like my first small condo that allowed me to start investing for just a few dollars). Don't worry about being right or wrong at first, just start. You'll learn a lot more once you put some money down . . . just a little to start. Money has a way of increasing intelligence quickly. Fear and hesitation retards you. You can always move up to a bigger game, but you can never get back the time and education you lost by waiting to do the right thing or make the big deal. Remember, small deals often lead to bigger deals . . . but you must start.

Start today, don't wait. Cut up your credit cards, get rid of 'doodads' and call a good no-load mutual fund (although there is no such thing as a true 'no-load' fund). Sit down with your loved ones and work out a plan, call a financial planner or go to the library and read about financial planning, and start putting money away (even if it's only $50 a month) for yourself. The longer you wait, the more you waste one of your most precious assets . . . the intangible and priceless asset of time.

An interesting note. Level 4 is where most of the millionaires in America come from. The book *The Millionaire Next Door* describes average millionaires as driving a Ford Taurus, owning a company and living within their means. They study or are informed about investing, have a plan, and invest for the long term. They do nothing fancy, risky or sexy when it comes to investing. They are truly conservative and their well-balanced financial habits are what make them rich and successful over the long haul.

For people who don't like risk, and would rather focus on their profession, job or career, instead of spending a lot of time studying the subject of investing, Level 4 is a must if you want to live a prosperous and financially abundant life. For these individuals, it is even more important to seek the advice of financial planners. They can help you develop your investment strategy and get you started on the right track with a long-term investing pattern.

This level of investor is patient and uses the advantage of time. If you start early and invest regularly, you can make it to phenomenal wealth. If you start late in life, past age 45, this level may not work, especially between now and the year 2010.

Do you know any Level 4 investors? (optional)

_____

_____

Level 5: Sophisticated Investors

These investors can 'afford' to seek more aggressive or risky investment strategies. Why? Because they have good money habits, a solid foundation of money and also investment savvy. They are not new to the game. They are focused, not usually diversified. They have a long track record of winning on a consistent basis, and they have had enough losses that give them the wisdom that only comes from making mistakes and learning from them.

These are the investors that often buy investments 'wholesale' rather than 'retail.' They put their own deals together for their own use. Or they are 'sophisticated' enough to get into deals that their Level 6 friends have put together that need investment capital.

What determines whether people are 'sophisticated?' They have a financial base that is sound, from their profession, business or retirement income, or have a base of solid, conservative investments. These people have their personal debt/equity ratios in control, which means they have much more income than expenses. They are well educated in the world of investing and actively seek new information. They are cautious, yet not cynical, always keeping an open mind.

They risk less than 20 percent of all their capital in speculative ventures. They often start small, putting a little money down, so they can learn the business of investing, be it stocks, a business acquisition, a real estate syndication, buying foreclosures, etc. If they lost this 20 percent, it would not damage them or take food off their table. They will look at the loss as a lesson, learn from it, and get back into the game to learn more, knowing that failure is part of the process of success. While hating to lose, they are not afraid of losing. Losing inspires them to move forward, to learn, rather than to dive into their emotional cave and call their attorney.

If people are sophisticated, they can create their own deals with returns of 25 percent to infinity. They are classified as sophisticated because they have the extra money, a team of hand-picked professional advisers, and a track record to prove it.

As mentioned earlier, investors at this level put their own deals together. Just as there are some who buy computers right off the retailer's shelf, there are some people who buy components and create their own customized computer system. Level 5 investors can assemble their investments by bringing different components together.

These investors know that bad economic times or markets offer them the best opportunities for success. They get into markets when others are getting out. They usually know when to get out. At this level, an exit strategy is more important than entry into the market.

They are clear on their own 'principles' and their 'rules' of investing. Their vehicle of choice might be real estate, discounted paper, businesses, bankruptcies or new issues of stocks. While they take risks greater than the average person, they abhor gambling. They have a plan and specific goals. They study on a daily basis. They read the paper, read magazines, subscribe to investment newsletters, and attend investment seminars. They actively participate in the management of their investments. They understand money and know how to have money work for them. Their main focus is on increasing their assets, rather than investing so they can make a few extra bucks to spend. They reinvest their gains to build a bigger asset base. They know that building a strong asset base that throws off high cash yields or high returns with minimal tax exposure is the path to great long-term wealth.

They often teach this information to their children and pass on the family fortune to the generations that follow in the form of corporations, trusts and partnerships. They personally own little. Nothing is found in their names for tax purposes as well as protection from Robin Hoods who believe in taking from the rich to give to the poor. But although they own nothing, they control everything through corporations. They control the legal entities that own their assets.

They have a personal board of directors to help them manage their assets. They take advice and learn. This informal board is comprised of a team of bankers, accountants, attorneys and brokers. They spend a small fortune on solid professional advice not only to increase their wealth but also to protect their wealth from family, friends, lawsuits and the government. Even after they have departed this life, they are still controlling their wealth. These people are often called 'stewards of money.' Even after death, they continue to direct the fate of the money they created.

Do you know any Level 5 investors? (optional)

_____

_____

Level 6: Capitalists

Few people in the world reach this level of investment excellence. In America, less than one person in a hundred is a true capitalist. This person is usually an excellent 'B' as well as an 'I' because he or she can create a business and an investment opportunity simultaneously.

A capitalist's purpose is to make more money by synergistically orchestrating other people's money, other people's talents, and other people's time. Often they are the 'movers and shakers' that allow America and other great countries to become great financial powers. These are the Kennedys, Rockefellers, Fords, J. Paul Gettys, and Ross Perots. It is the capitalists that provide the money that create the jobs, the businesses, and the goods that make a country prosper.

Level 5 investors generally create investments only for their own portfolio using their own money. True capitalists, on the other hand, create investments for themselves and others by using the talents and finances of other people. True capitalists create investments and sell them to the market. True capitalists do not need money to make money simply because they know how to use other people's money and other people's time. Level 6 investors create the investments that other people buy.

They often make other people rich, create jobs, and make things happen. In good economic times, true capitalists do well. In bad economic times, true capitalists get even richer. Capitalists know

117

that economic chaos means new opportunities. They are most often involved early in a project, product, company or country years before the masses find it popular. When you read in the paper about a country in trouble or in a war or a disaster, you can be assured that a true capitalist is going in soon, or may already be there. A true capitalist is going in while most people are saying, 'Stay away. That country, or that business, is in turmoil. It's too risky.'

Returns of 100 percent to infinity are expected. That's because they know how to manage risk and how to make money without money. They can do this because they know that money is not a thing, but merely an idea created in their head. While these people have the same fears everyone has, they use that fear and turn it into excitement. They convert fear into new knowledge and new wealth. Their game in life is the game of money making money. They love the game of money more than any other game . . . more than golf, gardening or goofing off. This is the game that gives them life. Whether they're winning or losing money, you can always hear them say, 'I love this game.' That's what makes them capitalists.

Like those at Level 5, investors at this level are also excellent 'stewards of money.' When studying most of the people at this level, you often find they are generous to their friends, family, churches and to education. Look at some of the famous people who founded our well known institutions of learning. Rockefeller helped create the University of Chicago, and J.P. Morgan influenced Harvard with more than money. Other capitalists who gave their names to the institutions they helped found include Vanderbilt, Duke and Stanford. They represent the great captains not only of industry but also of education.

Today, Sir John Templeton gives generously to religion and spirituality, and George Soros donates hundreds of millions to causes he believes in. Also don't forget the Ford Foundation and the Getty Foundation, and Ted Turner pledging a billion dollars to the United Nations.

So contrary to what many of the intellectual cynics and critics in our schools, government, churches and our media may say, true capitalists have contributed in more ways than just being captains of industry, providing jobs and making a lot of money. To create a better world, we need more capitalists, not fewer, as many cynics would have you believe.

In reality, there are many more cynics than capitalists. Cynics, who make more noise and keep millions of people in fear, seeking security instead of freedom. As my friend Keith Cunningham always says, 'I've never seen a statue erected to a cynic, or a university funded by a cynic.'

Do you know any Level 6 investors? (optional)

_____

_____

Before Reading Further

This completes the explanation part of the *CASHFLOW Quadrant*. This last chapter dealt with the 'I' section of the *Quadrant*. Before we go on, here is another question:

1. What level of investor are you? _____

If you are truly sincere about getting wealthy quickly, read and re-read the seven levels. Each time I read the levels, I see a little of myself in all the levels. I recognize not only strengths but also, as Zig Ziglar says, 'character flaws' that hold me back. The way to great financial wealth is to strengthen your strengths and address your character flaws. And the way to do that is by first recognizing them rather than pretending you are flawless.

We all want to think the best of ourselves. I have dreamed of being a Level 6 capitalist for most of my life. I knew this is what I wanted to become from the moment my rich dad explained the similarities between a stock picker and a person who bets on horses. But after studying the different levels of this list, I could see the character flaws that hold me back. Although I do operate today as a Level 6 investor, I continue to read and re-read the seven levels and work on improving myself.

I found character flaws in myself from Level 3-C that would often raise their ugly heads in times of pressure. The gambler in me was good, but it was also not good. So with the guidance of my wife and friends, and additional schooling, I immediately began addressing my own character flaws and turning them into strengths. My effectiveness as a Level 6 investor improved immediately.

Here's another question for you:

2. What level of investor do you want or need to be in the near future?

_____

If your answer to question No. 2 is the same as that in question No. 1, then you are where you want to be. If you are happy where you are, relative to being an investor, then there is not much need to read any further in this book. For example, if today you are a solid Level 4 investor and you have no desire to become a Level 5 or Level 6, then read no further. One of life's greatest joys is to be happy where you are. Congratulations!

> **WARNING**
>
> Anyone with the goal of becoming a Level 5 or 6 investor
> must develop their skills FIRST as a Level 4 investor. Level
> 4 cannot be skipped on your path to Level 5 or 6. Anyone
> who tries to become a Level 5 or 6 investor without the skills
> of a Level 4 investor is really a Level 3 investor . . . a Gambler!

If you still want and need to know more financially and continue to be interested in pursuing your financial freedom, read on. The remaining chapters will focus primarily on the characteristics of someone in the 'B' and 'I' quadrants. In these chapters, you will learn how to move from the left side of the *Quadrant* to the right side easily and with low risk. The shift from the left side to the right will continue to focus on intangible assets that make possible the tangible assets on the right side of the *Quadrant*.

Before going on, I have one last question: To go from home- less to millionaires in less than 10 years, what level of investor do you think Kim and I had to be? The answer is found in the next chapter, where I will share some learning experiences from my personal journey to financial freedom.

CHAPTER SIX

You Cannot See Money With Your Eyes

In late 1974, I purchased a small condominium on the fringes of Waikiki as one of my first investment properties. The price was $56,000 for a cute two-bedroom, one-bath unit in an average building. It was a perfect rental unit . . . and I knew it would rent quickly.

I drove over to my rich dad's office, all excited about showing him the deal. He glanced at the documents and in less than a minute he looked up and asked: 'How much money are you losing a month?'

'About $100 a month,' I said.

'Don't be foolish,' rich dad said. 'I haven't gone over the numbers, but I can already tell from the written documents that you're losing much more than that. And besides, why in the world would you knowingly invest in something that loses money?'

'Well, the unit looked nice, and I thought it was a good deal. A little paint and the place would be as good as new,' I said.

'That doesn't justify knowingly losing money,' smirked rich dad.

'Well, my real estate agent said not to worry about losing money every month. He said that in a few years the price of this unit will double, and in addition, the government gives me a tax break on the money I lose. Besides, it was such a good deal that I was afraid someone else would buy it if I didn't.'

Rich dad stood and closed his office door. When he did that, I knew I was about to be chewed out as well as be taught an important lesson. I had been through these types of educational sessions before.

'So how much money are you losing a month?' rich dad asked again.

'About $100 a month,' I repeated nervously.

Rich dad shook his head as he scanned the documents. The lesson was about to begin. On that day, I learned more about money and investing than I had in all my previous 27 years of life. Rich dad was happy that I had taken the initiative and invested in a property . . . but I had made some grave mistakes that could have been a financial disaster. However, the lessons I learned from that one investment have made me millions over the years.

Money Is Seen With Your Mind

'It's not what your eyes see,' said rich dad. 'A piece of real estate is a piece of real estate. A company's stock certificate is a company's stock certificate. You can see those things. But it's what you cannot see that is important. It's the deal, the financial agreement, the market, the management, the risk factors, the cash flow, the corporate structuring, the tax laws, and a thousand other things that make something a good investment or not.'

He then proceeded to tear the deal apart with questions. 'Why would you pay such a high interest rate? What do you figure your return on investment to be? How does this investment fit into your long-term financial strategy? What vacancy factor are you using? What is your cap rate? Have you checked the association's history of assessments? Have you figured in management costs?

124

What percentage rate did you use to compute repairs? Did you know that the city has just announced it will be tearing up the roads in that area and changing the traffic pattern? A major thoroughfare will run right in front of your building. Residents are moving to avoid the year-long project. Did you know that? I know the market trend is up today, but do you know what is driving that trend? Business economics or greed? How long do you think the trend will be up? What happens if this place is not rented? And if it isn't, how long can you keep it afloat and yourself afloat? And again, what goes on in your head to make you think that losing money is a good deal? This really has me worried.'

'It looked like a good deal,' I said, deflated.

Rich dad smiled, stood up and shook my hand. 'I'm glad you took action,' he said. 'Most people think, but never do. If you do something, you make mistakes, and it's from our mistakes that we learn the most. Remember that anything important cannot really be learned in the classroom. It must be learned by taking action, making mistakes, and then correcting them. That is when wisdom sets in.'

I felt a little better, and now I was ready to learn.

'Most people,' said rich dad, 'invest 95 percent with their eyes and only 5 percent with their minds.'

Rich dad went on to explain that people look at a piece of real estate, or the name of a stock, and often make their decision based on what their eyes see or what a broker tells them, or on a hot tip from a fellow worker. They often buy emotionally instead of rationally.

'That is why 9 out of 10 investors do not make money,' said rich dad. 'While they do not necessarily lose money, they just do not make money. They just sort of break even, making some and losing some. That's because they invest with their eyes and emotions, rather than with their minds. Many people invest because they want to get rich quickly. So instead of becoming

125

investors, they wind up being dreamers, hustlers, gamblers and crooks. The world is filled with them. So let's sit down, go back over this losing deal you just bought, and I will teach you how to turn it into a winning deal. I'll begin to teach your mind to see what your eyes cannot.'

From Bad To Good

The next morning, I went back to the real estate agent, rejected the agreement and reopened negotiation. It was not a pleasant process, but I learned a lot.

Three days later, I returned to see my rich dad. The price had stayed the same, the agent got his full commission because he deserved it. He had worked hard for it. But while the price remained the same, the terms of the investment were vastly different. By re-negotiating the interest rate, payment terms and the amortization period, instead of losing money, I was now certain of making a net profit of $80 per month, even after the management fee and an allowance for vacancy was factored in. I could even lower my rent, and still make money, if the market went bad. I would definitely raise the rent if the market got better.

'I estimated that you were going to lose at least $150 per month,' said rich dad. 'Probably more. If you had continued to lose $150 per month, based on your salary and expenses, how many of these deals could you afford?'

'Barely one,' I replied. 'Most months, I do not have an extra $150. If I had done the original deal, I would have struggled financially every month. Even after the tax breaks. I might even have had to take an extra job to pay for this investment.'

'And now, how many of these deals at $80 positive cash flow can you afford?' asked rich dad.

I smiled and said, 'As many as I can get my hands on.'

Rich dad nodded in approval. 'Now go out there and get your hands on more of them.'

A few years later, the real estate prices in Hawaii did skyrocket. But instead of having only one property go up in value, I had seven double in value. That is the power of a little financial intelligence.

'You Can't Do That'

An important side note to my first real estate investment: When I took my new offer back to the real estate agent, all he said to me was, 'You can't do that.'

What took the longest time was convincing the agent to start thinking about how we could do what I wanted done. In any event, there were many lessons I learned from this one investment, and one of those lessons was to realize that when someone says to you, 'You can't do that,' they may have one finger pointing forward at you . . . but three fingers are pointing backward at them.

Rich dad taught me 'You can't do that' doesn't necessarily mean 'you can't.' It more often means 'they can't.'

A classic example took place many years ago when people said to the Wright Brothers, 'You can't do that.' Thank goodness, the Wright Brothers did not listen.

$1.4 Trillion Looking For A Home

Every day, $1.4 trillion orbits the planet electronically, and it is increasing. There is more money being created and available today than ever before. The problem is, money is invisible. Today, the bulk of it is electronic. So when people look for money with their eyes, they fail to see anything. Most people struggle to live from paycheck to paycheck, and yet, $1.4 trillion flies around the world every day looking for someone who wants it. Looking for someone who knows how to take care of it, nurture it and grow it. If you know how to take care of money, money will flock to you, and be thrown at you. People will beg you to take it.

But if you do not know how to care for money, money will

stay away from you. Remember rich dad's definition of financial intelligence: 'It's not how much money you make, but how much money you keep, how hard it works for you, and how many generations you keep it for.'

The Blind Leading The Blind

'The average person is 95 percent eyes and only 5 percent mind when they invest,' said rich dad. 'If you want to become a professional on the 'B' and 'I' side of the *Quadrant*, you need to train your eyes to be only 5 percent and train your mind to see the other 95 percent. Rich dad went on to explain that people who trained their minds to see money had tremendous power over people who did not.

He was adamant about whom I took financial advice from. 'The reason most people struggle financially is because they take advice from people who are also mentally blind to money. It's the classic tale of the blind leading the blind. If you want money to come to you, you must know how to take care of it. If money is not first in your head, it will not stick to your hands. If it does not stick to your hands, then money, and people with money, will stay away from you.'

Train Your Brain To See Money

So what is the first step in training your brain to see money? The answer is easy. The answer is financial literacy. It begins with the ability to understand the words and the number systems of capitalism. If you do not understand the words or the numbers, you might as well be speaking a foreign language . . . and in many cases, each quadrant represents a foreign language.

If you look at the *CASHFLOW Quadrant*, each quadrant is like a different country. They do not all use the same words, and if you do not understand the words, you will not understand the numbers.

For example, if a medial doctor says, 'Your systolic is 120 and your diastolic is 80,' is that good or bad? Is that all you need to know for your health? The answer is obviously 'no.' Yet, it is a start.

It would be like asking, 'My stock's p/e is 12, and my apartment house cap rate is 12. Is this all I need to know for my wealth?' Again, the answer is 'no,' but it is a start. At least we're beginning to speak the same words and use the same numbers. And that is where financial literacy, which is the basis of financial intelligence, begins. It begins with knowing the words and numbers.

The doctor is speaking from the 'S' quadrant, and the other is speaking with the words and numbers of the 'I' quadrant. They might as well be different foreign languages.

I disagree when someone says to me, 'It takes money to make money.'

In my opinion, the ability to make money with money begins with understanding the words and numbers. As my rich dad always said, 'If money is not first in your head, it will not stick to your hands.'

Know What Real Risk Is

The second step in training your brain to see money is to learn to recognize what real risk is. When people say to me that investing is risky, I simply say, 'Investing is not risky. Being uneducated is risky.'

Investing is much like flying. If you've been to flight school and spent a number of years gaining experience, then flying is fun and exciting. But if you've never been to flight school, I would recommend leaving the flying to someone else.

Bad Advice Is Risky

Rich dad firmly believed that any financial advice was better than no financial advice. He was a man with an open mind. He was courteous and listened to many people. But ultimately, he relied on his own financial intelligence to make his decisions: 'If you do not know anything, then any advice is better than no advice. But if you cannot tell the difference between bad advice and good advice, then that is risky.'

Rich dad firmly believed that most people struggled financially because they operated on financial information handed down from parent to child . . . and most people do not come from financially sound families. 'Bad financial advice is risky, and most of the bad advice is handed out at home,' he often said. 'Not because of what is said, but because of what is done. Children learn by example more than words.'

Your Advisers Are Only As Smart As You

Rich dad said, 'Your advisers can only be as smart as you are. If you are not smart, they cannot tell you that much. If you are financially well educated, competent advisers can give you more sophisticated financial advice. If you are financially naive, they must by law offer you only safe and secure financial strategies. If you are an unsophisticated investor, they can only offer low-risk, low-yield investments. They'll often recommend 'diversification' for unsophisticated investors. Few advisers choose to take the time to teach you. Their time is also money. So if you will take it upon yourself to become financially educated and manage your money well, then a competent adviser can inform you about investments and strategies that only a few will ever see. But first, you must do your part to get educated. Always remember, your adviser can only be as smart as you.'

Is Your Banker Lying To You?

Rich dad had several bankers he dealt with. They were an important part of his financial team. While he was close friends with and respected his bankers, he always felt that he had to watch out for his own best interests . . . as he expected the bankers to look out for their own best interests.

After my 1974 investment experience, he asked me this: 'When a banker says that your house is an asset, are they telling you the truth?'

Since most people are not financially literate and do not know the game of money, they often must take the opinion and advice of people they tend to trust. If you are not financially literate, then you need to trust someone you hope is financially literate. Many people invest or manage their money based on someone else's recommendations more than their own. And that is risky.

They Are Not Lying . . .
They're Just Not Telling You The Truth

The fact is, when a banker tells you your house is an asset, they are not really lying to you. They're just not telling you the whole truth. While your house is an asset, they simply do not say whose asset it is. For if you read financial statements, it is easy to see that your house is not your asset. It's the bank's asset. Remember my rich dad's definitions of an asset and a liability from *Rich Dad, Poor Dad*:

'An asset puts money into my pocket.

A liability takes money out of my pocket.'

People on the left side of the *Quadrant* do not really need to know the difference. Most of them are happy to feel secure in their jobs, have a nice house they think they own, they feel proud of, and think they are in control of. Nobody will take it away from them as long as they make those payments. And make those payments they do.

But people on the right side of the *Quadrant* need to know the difference. To be financially literate and financially intelligent means being able to understand the big picture of money. Financially astute people know that a mortgage does not show up as an asset but as a liability on your balance sheet. Your mortgage actually shows up as an asset on a balance sheet across town. It shows up as an asset on the bank's balance sheet . . . not yours.

Your Balance Sheet

Assets	Liabilities
	Mortgage

Anyone who has taken accounting knows that a balance sheet must balance. But where does it balance? It does not really balance on your balance sheet. If you look at the bank's balance sheet, this is the story the numbers really tell.

Bank's Balance Sheet

Assets	Liabilities
Your Mortgage	

Now it balances. Now it makes sense. That is 'B and I' accounting. But this is not the way it is taught in basic accounting. In accounting, you would show the 'value' of your home as an asset and the mortgage as a liability. Also an important point to note is that the 'value' of your home is an opinion which fluctuates with the market while your mortgage is a definite liability not affected by the market. For a 'B and I,' however, the 'value' of your home is not considered an asset because it does not generate cash flow.

What Happens If You Pay Off Your Mortgage?

Many people ask me, 'What happens if I pay off my mortgage? Is my house an asset then?'

And my reply is, 'In most cases, the answer is still "no." It's still a liability.'

There are several reasons for my answer. One is maintenance and general upkeep. Property is like a car. Even if you own it free and clear, it still costs you money to operate . . . and once things start to break, everything begins to break. And in most cases, people pay for repairs on their house and their car with after-tax dollars. A person in the 'B and I' quadrants only includes property as an asset if it generates income through positive cash flow.

But the main reason a house, even without a mortgage, is still a liability is because you still do not own it . . . really. The government still taxes you even if you own it. Just stop paying your property taxes, and again you will find out who really owns your property.

That is where tax-lien certificates come from . . . which I wrote about in *Rich Dad, Poor Dad*. Tax-lien certificates are an excellent way to receive at least 16 percent interest on your money. If homeowners do not pay their property taxes, the government charges them interest on the taxes owed, at rates from 10 percent to 50 percent. Talk about usury. If you don't pay the property taxes, and someone like me pays them for you . . . then in many states, you owe me the taxes plus the interest. If you do not pay the taxes and the interest within a certain amount of time, I get to take your house just for the money I put up. In most states, property taxes take priority in repayment, even before the bank's mortgage. I have had the opportunity to buy houses I paid the taxes on for less than $3,500.

The Definition of Real Estate

Again, to be able to see money, you must see it with your mind, not your eyes. In order to train your mind, you must know the real definitions of words, and the system of numbers.

By now, you should know the difference between an asset and a liability, and you should know the definition of the word 'mortgage,' which is an 'agreement until death,' and the word 'finance,' which means penalty. You will now learn the origin of the words 'real estate' and a popular financial vehicle called 'derivatives.' Many people think 'derivatives' are new, but in reality, they are literally ages old.

A simple definition of 'derivative' is 'something that comes from something else.' An example of a derivative is orange juice. Orange juice is a derivative of an orange.

I used to think that real estate meant 'real' or something that was tangible. My rich dad explained to me that it really comes from the Spanish word real, which means 'royal.' El Camino Real means the royal's road. Real estate means the royal's estate.

Once the Agrarian Age came to an end and the Industrial Age began around 1500, the power was no longer based on the land and agriculture. The monarchs realized they had to change in response to the land-reform acts that allowed peasants to own the land. Then, the royalty created derivatives. Derivatives such as 'taxes' on land ownership and 'mortgages' as a way of allowing the commoners to finance their land. Taxes and mortgages are derivatives because they are derived from the land. Your banker would not call the mortgage a derivative; they would say it is 'secured' by the land . . . different words, similar meanings. So once the royalty realized that money was no longer in the land but in the 'derivatives' that came from the land, the monarchs set up banks to handle the increased business. Today, land is still called 'real estate' because no matter how much you pay for it, it never really belongs to you. It still belongs to the 'royals.'

What Is Your Interest Rate . . . Really?

Rich dad fought and negotiated tough for every single point of interest he paid. He asked me this question: 'When a banker tells you your interest rate is 8 percent per annum . . . is it really?' I found out it's not if you learn to read numbers.

Let's say you buy a $100,000 home, make a down payment of $20,000 and borrow the remaining $80,000 at 8 percent interest with a 30-year term from your bank.

In five years you will pay a total of $35,220 to the bank: $31,276 for interest, and only $3,944 for debt reduction.

If you take the loan to term, or 30 years, you will have paid

$211,323 total principal and interest, less what you originally borrowed – $80,000. The total interest you will have paid: $131,323.

By the way, that $211,323 does not include property taxes and insurance on the loan.

Funny, $131,323 seems to be a little bit more than 8 percent of $80,000. It's more like 160 percent in interest over 30 years. As I said, they are not lying . . . they are just not telling the whole truth. And if you cannot read numbers, you'd really never know. And if you're happy with your house, you'll never really care. But, of course, the industry knows that in a few years . . . you're going to want a new house, a bigger house, a smaller house, a vacation house, or to refinance your mortgage. They know it and, in fact, they count on it.

Industry Average

In the banking industry, a seven-year average is used as the life expectancy for a mortgage. That means, banks expect the average person to buy a new house, or refinance every seven years. And that means in this example, they expect to get their original $80,000 back every seven years, plus $43,291 in interest.

And that's why it is called a 'mortgage,' which comes from the French word 'mortir' or 'agreement until death.' The reality is that most people will continue to work hard, get pay raises and buy new houses . . . with new mortgages. On top of that, the government gives a tax break to encourage taxpayers to buy more expensive houses, which will mean higher property taxes for the government. And let's not forget the insurance that every mortgage company requires you to pay on your mortgage.

Every time I watch television, I see commercials where handsome professional baseball and football players smile and tell you to take all your credit card debt and roll it into a 'bill consolidation loan.' That way, you can pay off all those credit cards and carry a new loan at a lower interest rate. And then they tell you why it's financially intelligent to do this: 'A bill consolidation loan is a smart move on your part because the government will give you a tax deduction for the interest payments you make on your home mortgage.'

Viewers, thinking they see the light, run down to their finance company, refinance their houses, pay off their credit cards and feel intelligent.

A few weeks later, they're shopping and see a new dress, a new lawn mower, or realize their kid needs a new bicycle, or they need to take a vacation because they're exhausted. They just happen to now have a clean credit card . . . or they suddenly receive a new credit card in the mail because they paid off the other one. They have excellent credit, they pay their bills, their little heart goes pitter-patter, and they say to themselves, 'Oh, go on. You deserve it. You can pay it off a little every month.'

Emotions overpower logic, and the clean new credit card comes out of hiding.

As I said, when bankers say your house is an asset . . . they aren't lying. When the government gives you a tax break for being in debt, it isn't because it's concerned about your financial future. The government is concerned about its financial future. So when your banker, your accountant, your attorney and your school-teachers tell you your house is an asset, they just failed to say whose asset it is.

What About Savings? Are They Assets?

Now, your savings really are assets. That's the good news. But again, if you read financial statements, you will see the total picture. While it is true that your savings are assets, when you look across town at the bank's balance sheet, your savings show up as a liability. This is what your savings and checkbook balance look like in your asset column.

Your Balance Sheet

Assets	Liabilities
Savings	
Checkbook Balance	

And this is how your savings and your checkbook balance are carried on your bank's balance sheet.

Bank's Balance Sheet

Assets	Liabilities
	Your Savings
	Your Checkbook Balance

Why is your savings and checkbook balance a liability to banks? They have to pay you interest for your money, and it costs them money to safeguard it.

If you can get the significance of these few drawings and words, you might begin to better understand what the eyes cannot see about the game of money.

Why You Don't Get A Tax Break For Saving Money?

If you notice, you get a tax break for buying a house and going into debt . . . but you do not get a tax break for saving money. Have you ever wondered why?

I do not have the exact answer, but I can speculate. One big reason is because your savings are a liability to banks. Why would they ask the government to pass a law that would encourage you to put money in their bank . . . money that would be a liability to them?

They Don't Need Your Savings

Besides, banks really do not need your savings. They don't need much in deposits because they can magnify money at least 10 times. If you put a single $1 note in the bank, by law, the bank can lend out $10 and, depending upon the reserve limits imposed by the central bank, possibly as much as $20. That means your single $1 suddenly becomes $10 or more. It's magic! When my rich dad showed me that, I fell in love with the idea. At that point I knew that I wanted to own a bank, and not go to school to become a banker.

On top of that, the bank might pay you only 5 percent interest on that $1. You as a consumer feel secure because the bank is paying you some money on your money. Banks see this as good customer relations, because if you have savings with them, you may come in and borrow from them. They want you to borrow because they can then charge 9 percent or more to you on what you borrow. While you may make 5 percent on your $1, the bank can make 9 percent or more on the $10 of debt your single dollar has generated. Recently, I received a new credit card that advertised 8.9 percent interest . . . but if you understood the legal jargon in the fine print, it was really 23 percent. Needless to say, that credit card was cut in half and mailed back.

They Get Your Savings Anyway

The other reason they don't offer a tax break for savings is more obvious. If you can read the numbers and see which way the cash is flowing, you'll notice that they'll get your savings anyway. The money you could be saving in your asset column is flowing instead out of your liability column, in the form of interest payments on your mortgage in their asset column. The cash flow pattern looks like this:

Your Financial Statement

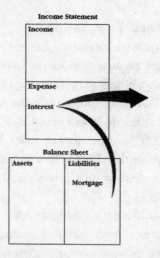

Your Bank's Financial Statement

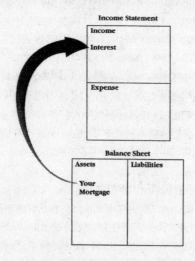

That is why they don't need the government to give you a tax incentive to save. They'll get your savings anyway . . . in the form of interest payments on debt.

Politicians are not about to mess with the system because the banks, insurance companies, building industry, brokerage houses and others contribute a lot of money to political campaigns . . . and the politicians know the name of the game.

The Name Of The Game

In 1974, my rich dad was upset because the game was played against me, and I did not know it. I had bought this investment real estate and had taken a losing position . . . yet, I had been led to believe it was a winning position.

'I'm glad you entered the game,' said rich dad. 'But because no one has ever told you what the game is, you've just been suckered over to the losing team.'

Rich dad then explained the basics of the game. 'The name of the game of capitalism is "Who is indebted to whom?"'

Once I knew the game, he said, then I could be a better player . . . instead of someone who just had the game run all over them.

The More People You Are Indebted To, The Poorer You Are

'The more people you are indebted to, the poorer you are,' said rich dad. 'And the more people you have indebted to you, the wealthier you are. That is the game.'

As I said, I struggled to keep my mind open. So I stayed silent and let him explain. He was not saying it maliciously; he was just explaining the game as he saw it.

'We are all in debt to someone else. The problems occur when the debt gets out of balance. Unfortunately, the poor people of this world have been run over so hard by the game, they often can't get any deeper into debt. The same is true for poor countries. The world simply takes from the poor, the weak, the financially uninformed. If you have too much debt, the world takes everything you have . . . your time, your work, your home, your life, your confidence, and then they take your dignity, if you let them. I did not make up this game, I do not make the rules, but I do know the game . . . and I play the game well. I will explain the game to you. I want you to learn to play the game. Then, after you've mastered the game, you can decide what to do with what you know.'

Money Is Debt

Rich dad went on to explain that even our currency is not an instrument of equity, but an instrument of debt. Every dollar bill used to be backed by gold or silver, but is now an IOU guaranteed to be paid by the taxpayers of the issuing country. As long as the rest of the world has confidence in the American taxpayer to work and pay for this IOU called money, the world will have confidence in our dollar. If that key element of money, which is 'confidence,' suddenly disappears, the economy comes down like a house of cards . . . and the house of cards has come down many times throughout history.

Take the example of the German Weimar-government marks that became utterly worthless just before World War II. As one story goes, this elderly woman was pushing a wheelbarrow full of marks to buy a loaf of bread. When she turned her back, someone stole the wheelbarrow and left the pile of worthless money all over the street.

That is why most money today is known as 'fiat' money, which is money that cannot be converted to something tangible . . . like gold or silver. The money is only as good as long as people have confidence in the government backing it. The other definition for 'fiat' is a 'dictatorial order or decree given by a person or group having complete authority.'

142

Today, much of the global economy is based on debt and confidence. As long as we all keep holding hands, and no one breaks ranks, everything will be fine . . . and the word 'fine' is my acronym for, Feeling Insecure Neurotic and Emotional.

'Who Owes You?'

Going back to 1974, when I was learning how to buy that $56,000 condo, my rich dad taught me an important lesson on how to structure deals.

'"Who is indebted to whom?" is the name of the game,' said rich dad. 'And somebody just stuck you with the debt. It's like going to dinner with 10 friends. You go to the restroom and when you come back, the bill is there, but all 10 friends are gone. If you're going to play the game, then you had best learn the game, know the rules, speak the same language, and know with whom you're playing. If not, instead of playing the game, the game will be played on you.'

It's Only A Game

At first I got angry at what my rich dad told me . . . but I listened and did my best to understand. Finally he put it into a context that I could understand. 'You love playing football, don't you?' he asked.

I nodded my head. 'I love the game,' I said.

'Well, money is my game,' said rich dad. 'I love the money game.'

'But for many people, money is not a game,' I said.

'That is correct,' said rich dad. 'For most people, it's survival. For most people, money is a game they are forced to play, and they hate it. Unfortunately, the more civilized we get, the more money becomes a part of our lives.'

Rich dad drew the *CASHFLOW Quadrant.*

'Just look at this as a tennis court, or football field, or soccer field. If you're going to play the money game, which team do you want to be on? The 'E's, S's, B's or I's'? Or which side of the court do you want to be on – the right side or the left?'

I pointed to the right side of the *Quadrant*.

If You Take On Debt And Risk, You Should Be Paid

'Good,' said rich dad. 'That is why you cannot go out there to play the game and believe some sales agent when he tells you that to lose $150 a month for 30 years is a good deal . . . because the government will give you a tax break for losing money and he expects the price of real estate to go up. You simply cannot play the game with that mind-set. While those opinions might come true, that is just not the way the game is played on the right side of the *Quadrant*. Somebody is telling you to get into debt, take all the risks, and pay for it. People on the left side think that is a good idea . . . but not the people on the right.'

I was shaking a little.

'Look at it my way,' said rich dad. 'You're willing to pay $56,000 for this condo in the sky. You're signing for the debt. You take the

144

risk. The tenant pays less in rent than what it costs to live there. So you are subsidizing that person's housing. Does that make sense to you?'

I shook my head. 'No.'

'This is the way I play the game,' said rich dad. 'From now on, if you take on debt and risk, then you should get paid. Got that?'

I nodded my head.

'Making money is common sense,' said rich dad. 'It's not rocket science. But unfortunately, when it comes to money, common sense is uncommon. A banker tells you to take on debt, tells you that the government will give you a tax break for something that really does not make fundamental economic sense, and then a real estate sales person tells you to sign the papers because he can find a tenant who will pay you less than you are paying, just because in his opinion the price will go up. If that makes sense to you, then you and I do not share the same common sense.'

I just stood there. I heard everything he said, and I had to admit that I had gotten so excited by what I thought looked like a good deal that my logic went out of the window. I could not analyze the deal. Because the deal 'looked' good, I had gotten emotional with greed and excitement, and I was no longer able to hear what the numbers and the words were trying to tell me.

It was then that rich dad gave me an important rule that he has always used, 'Your profit is made when you buy . . . not when you sell.'

Rich dad had to be certain that whatever debt or risk he took on, it had to make sense from the day he bought it . . . it had to make sense if the economy got worse, and it had to make sense if the economy got better. He never bought on tax tricks or crystal ball forecasts of the future. A deal had to make sound economic sense in good times and in bad.

I was beginning to understand the game of money as he saw

it. And the game of money was to see others become indebted to you and to be careful whom you became indebted to. Today, I still hear his words: 'If you take on risk and debt, make sure you get paid for it.'

Rich dad had debt, but he was careful when he took it on. 'Be careful when you take on debt,' was his advice. 'If you take on debt personally, make sure it's small. If you take on large debt, make sure someone else is paying for it.'

He saw the game of money and debt as a game that is played on you, played on me, played on everyone. It's played from business to business, and it's played from country to country. He saw it only as a game. The problem is, for most people, money is not a game. For many people, money is survival . . . often life itself. And because no one explained the game to them, they still believe bankers who say a house is an asset.

The Importance Of Facts Versus Opinions

Rich dad continued his lesson: 'If you want to be successful on the right side, when it comes to money, you have got to know the difference between facts and opinions. You cannot blindly accept financial advice the way people on the left side do. You must know the numbers. You must know the facts. And numbers tell you the facts. Your financial survival depends upon facts, not some friend or adviser's wordy opinions.

'I don't understand. What is the big deal about something being a fact or opinion?' I asked. 'Is one better than the other?'

'No,' replied rich dad. 'Just know when something is a fact and when something is an opinion.'

Still puzzled I stood there with a confused look on my face.

'What is your family's home worth?' asked rich dad. He was using an example to help me out of my confusion.

'Oh I know,' I replied quickly. 'My parents are thinking about selling so they had a real estate agent come in and give us an appraisal. They said the house was worth $36,000. That means my dad's net worth increased by $16,000 because he only paid $20,000 for it 5 years ago.'

'So is the appraisal and your dad's net worth a fact or an opinion?' asked rich dad.

I thought about it for a while and understood what he was getting at. 'Both are opinions. Aren't they?'

Rich dad nodded his head. 'Very good. Most people struggle financially because they spend their lives using opinions rather than facts when making financial decisions. Opinions such as 'Your house is an asset.' 'The price of real estate always goes up.' 'Blue chip stocks are your best investment.' 'It takes money to make money.' 'Stocks have always out performed real estate.' 'You should diversify your portfolio.' 'You have to be dishonest to be rich.' 'Investing is risky.' 'Play it safe.'

I sat there deep in thought, realizing that most of what I heard about money at home was really people's opinions, not facts.

'Is gold an asset?' asked rich dad, snapping me out of my daydream.

'Yes. Of course.' I replied. 'It has been the only real money that has withstood the test of time.'

'See there you go again.' smiled rich dad. 'All you are doing is repeating someone else's opinion about what is an asset rather than checking out the facts.'

'Gold is only an asset, by my definition, if you buy it for less than you sell it for,' rich dad said slowly. 'In other words, if you bought it for $100 and sold it for $200, then it was an asset. But if you bought one ounce for $200 and you sold it for $100 then gold in this transaction was a liability. It's the actual financial numbers of the transaction that ultimately tell you the facts. In reality, the only thing that is an asset or liability is you . . . for ultimately it is you that can make gold an asset and only you can make it a liability. That is why financial education is so important.

I have seen so many people take a perfectly good business, or piece of real estate and turn it into a financial nightmare. Many people do the same with their personal life. They take hard earned money and create a lifetime of financial liabilities.'

I was even more confused, a little hurt inside, and wanted to argue. Rich dad was toying with my brain.

'Many a man has been suckered because he did not know the facts. Everyday I hear horror stories of someone who lost all their money because they thought an opinion was a fact. It's OK to use an opinion when making a financial decision . . . but you'd best know the difference. Millions upon millions of people have made life decisions based upon opinions handed down from generation to generation . . . and then they wonder why they struggle financially.'

'What kind of opinions?' I asked.

Rich dad chuckled to himself before he answered. 'Well, let me give you a few common ones we have all heard.'

Rich dad began listing a few as he chuckled quietly, apparently laughing at the humor of being human beings. Some of the examples he gave that day were:

1. 'You should marry him. He'll make a good husband.'
2. 'Find a secure job and stay there all your life.'
3. 'Doctors make a lot of money.'
4. 'They have a big house. They must be rich.'
5. 'He has big muscles. He must be healthy.'
6. 'This is a nice car, only driven by a little old lady.'
7. 'There is not enough money for everyone to be rich.'
8. 'The earth is flat.'
9. 'Humans will never fly.'
10. 'He's smarter than his sister.'
11. 'Bonds are safer than stocks.'
12. 'People who make mistakes are stupid.'

13. 'He'll never sell for such a low price.'
14. 'She'll never go out with me.'
15. 'Investing is risky.'
16. 'I'll never be rich.'
17. 'I didn't go to college so I'll never get ahead.'
18. 'You should diversify your investments.'
19. 'You shouldn't diversify your investments.'

Rich dad went on and on until finally he could tell I was tired of hearing his examples of opinions.

'OK!' I finally said. 'I've heard enough. What is your point?'

'Thought you'd never stop me,' smiled rich dad. 'The point is most people's lives are determined by their opinions, rather than the facts. For a person's life to change, they first need to change their opinions . . . then start looking at the facts. If you can read financial statements, you will be able to see the facts not only of a company's financial success . . . if you can read financial statements you can tell immediately how an individual is doing . . . rather than going by yours or somebody else's opinions. As I said, one is not better than the other. To be successful in life, especially financially, you must know the difference. If you cannot verify something is a fact, then it is an opinion. Financial blindness is when a person cannot read numbers . . . so they must take someone else's opinion. Financial insanity is caused when opinions are used as facts. If you want to be on the right side of the *Quadrant*, you must know the difference between facts and opinions. Few lessons are more important than this one.'

I sat there listening quietly doing my best to understand what he was saying. It was obviously a simple concept yet it was larger than my brain could accept at that moment.

'Do you know what "due diligence" means?' rich dad asked.

I shook my head.

'Due diligence simply means finding out what are opinions and what are facts. When it comes to money, most people are either lazy or searching for shortcuts, so they do not do enough due diligence. And there are still others who are so afraid of making mistakes that all they do is due diligence and then do nothing. Too much due diligence is also called "analysis paralysis". The point is you must know how to sift through the facts and opinions, and then make your decision. As I said, most people are in financial trouble today simply because they've taken too many shortcuts and are making their life's financial decisions based upon opinions, often the opinions of an 'E' or an 'S', and not the facts. If you want to be a 'B' or an 'I', you must be keenly aware of this difference.'

I did not fully appreciate rich dad's lesson that day, yet few lessons have served me better than to know the difference between facts and opinions, especially when it comes to handling my money.

Years later, in the early 1990's, my rich dad watched the stock market climb out of sight. His only comment was,

'That is what happens when highly paid employees or self-employed people, with big pay checks, paying excessive amounts in taxes, greatly in debt, and with only paper assets in their portfolio begin handing out investment advice. Millions are about to get hurt following the opinions of people who think they know the facts.'

Warren Buffet, America's greatest investor, once said,

'If you are in a poker game and after 20 minutes you do not know who the patsy is, then you're the patsy.'

Why People Struggle Financially

I heard recently that most people will be in debt from the day they leave school until the day they die.

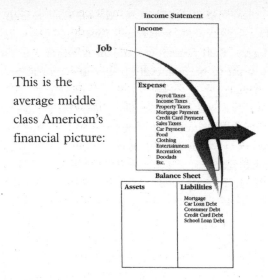

This is the average middle class American's financial picture:

Someone Else's Balance Sheet

If you now understand the game, then you may realize that those liabilities listed must show up on someone else's balance sheet like this.

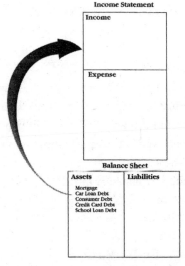

Anytime you hear these words, 'Low down, easy monthly payments,' or 'Don't worry, the government will give you a tax break for those losses,' then you know someone is luring you into the game. If you want to be financially free, you've got to be a little smarter than that.

For most people, no one is indebted to them. They have no real assets (things that put money in their pocket) . . . and they are often indebted to everyone else. That is why they cling to job security and struggle financially. If it were not for their job, they'd be broke in a flash. It has been said that the average American is less than three paychecks away from bankruptcy, just because they sought a better life and got run over by the game. The deck is stacked against them. They still think their house, car, golf clubs, clothes, vacation home, and other doodads are assets. They believed what someone else told them. They have to believe it because they cannot read financial numbers. They cannot tell facts from opinions. Most people go to school and learn to be players in the game, but no one explained the game to them. No one told them that the name of the game is 'Who is indebted to whom?' And because no one told them that, they're the ones who become indebted to everyone else.

Money Is An Idea

I hope you now understand the basics of the *CASHFLOW Quadrant* and know that money really is an idea that is more clearly seen with your mind than your eyes. Learning the game of money and how it is played is an important part of your journey to financial freedom. More important, though, is who you need to become to move to the right side of the *CASHFLOW Quadrant*. Part II of this book will focus on 'Bringing Out The Best In You' and in analyzing the formula:

Be-Do-Have

PART TWO

BRINGING OUT THE BEST IN YOU

CHAPTER SEVEN

Becoming Who You Are

'It's not being homeless that matters,' my rich dad said. 'It's about who you are. Keep striving and you become somebody. Quit and you also become somebody . . . but not the same person.'

The Changes You Go Through

For those of you contemplating going from job security to financial security, all I can offer you are words of encouragement. For Kim and me, it took being homeless and desperate before I found the courage to move forward. That was our path, but it definitely does not have to be your path. As I described earlier, there are ready-made systems that can help you cross the bridge to the right side of the *Quadrant*.

The real issue is the changes you go through internally and who you become in the process. For some people, the process is easy. For others, the journey is impossible.

Money Is A Drug

Rich dad would always say to Mike and me, 'Money is a drug.'

The main reason he refused to pay us while we worked for him was because he never wanted us to become addicted to working for money. 'If you become addicted to money,' he said, 'it's hard to break that addiction.'

When I was calling him from California as a grown man to ask him for money, he was not about to break a pattern he had started with Mike and me when we were 9. He did not give us money as kids, and he was not about to start now. Instead he continued to be tough and guide me away from the addiction of working for money.

He called money a drug because he had observed people who were happy when they had money, and upset or moody when they did not. Just as heroine addicts get high when they inject the drug, they also get moody and violent when they don't have it.

'Be careful of money's addictive power,' he often said. 'Once you get used to receiving it, that addiction keeps you attached to the way you got it.'

Put another way, if you receive money as an employee, then you tend to get accustomed to that way of acquiring it. If you get used to generating money by being self-employed, it is often difficult to break the attachment to earning money in that way. And if you get used to government handouts, that, too, is a hard pattern to break.

'The hardest part about moving from the left side to the right side is the attachment you have to the way you have been earning money,' said rich dad. 'It's more than breaking a habit; it's breaking an addiction.'

That is why he stressed to Mike and me to never work for money. He insisted we learn to create our own systems as a way of acquiring money.

The Patterns

For Kim and me, the hardest part in trying to become people who generated income in the 'B' quadrant was that all of our past conditioning was still holding us back. It was tough when friends said, 'Why are you doing this? Why don't you just get a job?'

It was even more difficult because there was a part of us that also wanted to go back to the security of a paycheck.

Rich dad explained to Mike and me that the world of money was one large system. And we as individuals learn how to operate in certain patterns within that system. For example:

An 'E' works for the system.

An 'S' is the system.

A 'B' creates, owns or controls the system.

An 'I' invests money into the system.

The pattern rich dad was talking about was the pattern in our body, mind and soul of how we naturally gravitate to the subject of money.

'When a person feels the need for money,' rich dad explained, 'an "E" will automatically look for a job, an "S" often will do something alone, a "B" will create or buy a system that produces money, and an "I" will look for an opportunity to invest in an asset that produces more money.'

Why It's Hard To Change A Pattern

'The reason it's hard to change a pattern,' said rich dad, 'is because money today is essential for life. In the Agrarian Age, money was not that important because the land could provide food, shelter, warmth and water without money. Once we moved into the cities during the Industrial Age, money signified life itself. Today, even water costs money.'

Rich dad went on to explain that when you begin to move from, let's say, the 'E' quadrant to the 'B' quadrant, the part of you that is addicted to being an 'E,' or afraid that life will end, begins to kick and fight back. It's like a drowning person beginning to fight for air, or a starving man who will eat anything to survive.

'It's this battle that goes on inside of you that makes it so hard. It's the battle between who you no longer are and who you want to become that is the problem,' rich dad explained to me over the phone. 'The part of you that still seeks security is in a war with that part of you that wants freedom. Only you can decide which one will win. You'll either build that business or you'll go back to finding a job-forever.'

Find Your Passion

'Do you really want to move forward?' asked rich dad.

'Yes!' I said hurriedly.

'Have you forgotten what you set out to do? Have you forgotten about your passion and what caused you to get into this predicament in the first place?' asked rich dad.

'Oh,' I replied, a little startled. I had forgotten. So I stood there at the pay phone, clearing my head so I could remember what got me into this mess in the first place.

'I knew it,' said rich dad, his voice booming over the phone. 'You're more worried about your own personal survival than keeping your dream alive. Your fear has pushed aside your passion. The best way to keep going is to keep the flame in your heart going. Always remember what you set out to do, and the trip will be easy. Start worrying more about yourself, and your fear begins to eat away at your soul. Passion builds businesses. Not fear. You've gone this far. You're close, so don't turn back now. Remember what you set out to do, keep that memory in your heart and keep the flame going. You can always quit . . . so why quit now?'

With that, rich dad wished me luck and hung up the phone.

He was correct. I had forgotten why I set out on this journey. I had forgotten about my dream and allowed my fears to fill my head as well as my heart.

Just a few years earlier, there had been a movie entitled 'Flash

Dance.' The theme song said something about, 'Take your passion and make it happen.'

Well, I had forgotten my passion. It was now time to make it happen or go back home and forget about it. I stood there for a while, and again I heard rich dad's last words: 'You can always quit. So why quit now?'

I decided to delay quitting until I had made things happen.

Becoming A Teacher Who Owned The System

I stood at the phone booth after rich dad and I had hung up. My fears and lack of success were beating me, and my dream had been pushed aside. My dream of creating a different kind of school system. An educational program for people who wanted to be entrepreneurs and investors. As I stood there, my mind drifted back to my days in high school.

When I was 15 years old, my high school guidance counselor asked me, 'What are you going to do when you grow up? Are you going to become a teacher like your dad?'

Looking straight at my counselor, my answer was straightforward, strong and filled with conviction. 'I'll never be a teacher. Becoming a teacher is the last thing I would ever do.'

I did not dislike school. I hated it. I absolutely hated being forced to sit and listen to someone I did not particularly like or respect speak for months on a subject I had no interest in. I fidgeted, squirmed, caused problems in the back of the room, unless I just left instead of going to class.

So when my guidance counselor asked me if I was planning to seek a career, following in my father's footsteps as a teacher, I nearly jumped out of my skin.

Little did I know at the time that passion is a combination of love and hate. I loved learning, but I hated school. I absolutely detested sitting there and being programmed into becoming something I did not want to be. I was not alone.

Notable Quotes On Education

Winston Churchill once said: 'I am always ready to learn, but I do not always like being taught.'

John Updike said: 'The founding fathers in their wisdom decided that children were an unnatural strain on their parents. So they provided jails called school, equipped with tortures called education.'

Norman Douglas said: 'Education is the state-controlled manufactory of echoes.'

H.L. Mencken said: 'School days, I believe, are the unhappiest in the whole span of human existence. They are full of dull, unintelligible tasks, new and unpleasant ordinances, and brutal violations of common sense and common decency.'

Galileo said: 'You cannot teach a person anything; you can only help him find it within himself.'

Mark Twain said: 'I never let schooling interfere with my education.'

Albert Einstein said: 'There is too much education altogether, especially in American schools.'

A Gift From My Educated Dad

The person who shared these quotes with me was my highly educated but poor dad. He also despised the school system . . . although he did well in it. He became a teacher because he had dreams of changing the 300 year old system, but instead, the system crushed him. He took his passion, tried to change the system, and ran into a brick wall. It was a system that too many people were making money in, and no one wanted it changed . . . although there was a lot of talk about the need for change.

Maybe my guidance counselor was psychic because years later I did indeed follow in my father's footsteps. I just didn't follow him into the same system. I was taking that same passion and creating my own system. That is why I was homeless. My passion was to create an educational system that taught people differently.

When my educated dad learned that Kim and I were struggling financially, doing our best to set up our own educational system, he sent us those quotes. Scribbled across the top of the page of the quotes were these words:

'Keep going.' Love, Dad.

Up until that moment, I never knew how much my educated dad had hated the system and what it did to young people. But after this gesture of encouragement, things began to make sense. The passion that was driving me then was the same passion that had driven him years earlier. I was just like my real dad, and I had unwittingly picked up the torch from him. I was a teacher at the core . . . maybe that is why I hated the system so much.

In hindsight, I had become both dads. From my rich dad, I had learned the secrets of being a capitalist. From my highly educated dad, I inherited the passion for teaching. And given the combination of the two dads, I could now do something about the educational system. I did not have the desire or ability to change the current system. But I did have the knowledge to create my own system.

The Years Of Training Begin To Pay Off

For years, my rich dad groomed me to be a person who created businesses and business systems. The business I set up, in 1977, was a manufacturing company. We were one of the first companies to produce the nylon and velcro 'surfer wallets' that came in bright colors. We followed that product with the 'shoe pocket' – a miniature wallet, also made of nylon and velcro, that attached to the shoe laces of running shoes. In 1978, jogging was the new craze, and joggers always wanted a place to put their keys, and to carry money or ID cards in case they got hurt. That is why I designed the 'shoe pocket' and marketed it to the world.

Our meteoric success was phenomenal, but soon the passion for the product line and the business drifted away. It began to weaken once my little company began to be pounded by foreign competition. Countries like Taiwan, Korea and Hong Kong were shipping products identical to mine and were wiping out the markets we had developed. Their prices were so low that there was no way we could compete. They were retailing products for less than it cost us to manufacture them.

Our little company was faced with a dilemma: fight them or join them. The partners realized we could not fight the competition. The companies flooding the market with cheap products were too strong. A vote was taken, and we decided to join them.

The tragedy was, in order to stay afloat, we had to let go of most of our faithful and hard-working staff. That broke my heart. When I went over to inspect the new factories we contracted with for our manufacturing in Korea and Taiwan, again my soul died a little. The conditions these young workers were forced to work in were cruel and inhumane. I saw five workers stacked one on top of the other, in a space where we would only allow one worker. My conscience began to bother me deeply. Not only for the workers we let go in America, but for the workers overseas who were now working for us.

Although we had solved the financial problem of foreign competition and began to make a lot of money, my heart was no longer in the business . . . and the business began to sag. Its spirit was gone because my spirit was gone. I no longer wanted to become rich if it meant exploiting so many low-paid workers. I began to think about educating people to be owners of businesses, not employees of business. At the age of 32, I was beginning to become a teacher, but didn't realize it at the time. The business began to decline not due to a lack of systems but because of a lack of heart, or passion. By the time Kim and I started out on our new business venture, the wallet company was gone.

Downsizing Coming

In 1983, I was invited to give a talk to the MBA class at the University of Hawaii. I gave them my views on job security. They did not like what I said: 'In a few years, many of you will lose your jobs, or be forced to work for less and less money, with less and less security.'

Because my work caused me to travel the world, I witnessed firsthand the combined power of cheap labor and innovations from technology. I began to realize that a worker in Asia or Europe or Russia or South America was really competing with workers in America. I knew the idea of high pay and a safe, secure job for workers and middle managers was an idea whose time had past. Big companies would soon have to make cuts, both in the numbers of people and in the dollars they paid to workers, just to be able to compete globally.

I was never asked back to the University of Hawaii. A few years later, the word 'downsizing' became standard practice. Every time a big company merged, and workers became redundant, downsizing occurred. Every time the owners wanted to make their shareholders happy, a downsizing occurred. With each downsizing, I saw the people at the top get richer and richer, and the people at the bottom pay the price.

Every time I heard someone say, 'I'm sending my child to a good school so he or she can get a good safe, secure job,' I cringed. Being prepared for a job is a good idea for the short term, but it is not enough for the long term. Slowly but surely, I was becoming a teacher.

Build A System Around Your Passion

Although my manufacturing company had turned around and was doing well again, my passion was gone. My rich dad summed up my frustration when he said: 'School days are over. It's time to build a system around your heart. Build a system around your passion. Let the manufacturing company go and build what you know you must build. You have learned well from me, but you are still your father's son. You and your dad are teachers deep in your souls.'

Kim and I packed up everything and moved to California to learn new teaching methods, so we could create a business around those methods. Before we could get the business off the ground, we ran out of money and were out on the street. It was that phone call to my rich dad, my wife standing by me, anger at myself, and a rekindling of the passion, that got us out of the mess we were in.

Soon we were back at building a company. The company was an educational company using teaching methods almost exactly opposite of what traditional schools use. Instead of asking students to sit still, we encouraged them to be active. Instead of teaching via lecture, we taught by playing games. Instead of being boring, we insisted our teachers be fun. Instead of teachers, we sought out business people who had actually started their own companies, and taught our style of teaching. Instead of grading the students, the students graded the teacher. If the teacher got a lousy grade, the teacher was either put through another intensive training program, or asked to leave.

Age, educational background, sex and religious beliefs were not criteria. All we asked for was a sincere desire to learn and to learn quickly. We were eventually able to teach a year's worth of accounting in one day.

Although we mainly taught adults, we had many young people, some 16 years old, learning right alongside highly paid, well-educated 60 year old business executives. Instead of competing on tests, we asked them to cooperate on teams. Then, we had the team taking a test competing against other teams taking the same test. Instead of striving for grades, we bet money. Winner take all. The competition and desire to do well as a team was fierce. The teacher did not have to motivate the class. The teacher just had to get out of the way once the learning competition was on. Instead of quiet at test time, there was yelling, screaming, laughter and tears. People were excited about learning. They were 'turned on' by learning . . . and they wanted to learn more.

We focused on teaching just two subjects: entrepreneurship and investing. The 'B' and 'I' side of the *Quadrant*. The people who wanted to learn these subjects in our style of education showed up in droves. We did no advertising. Everything spread by word of mouth. The people who showed up were people who wanted to create jobs, not people looking for jobs.

Once I made up my mind not to quit that night at the phone booth, things began to move forward. In less than five years, we had a multimillion-dollar business with 11 offices throughout the world. We had built a new system of education, and the market loved it. Our passion had made it happen, because passion and a good system overcame fear and past programming.

A Teacher Can Be Rich

Whenever I hear teachers say they are not paid enough, I feel for them. The irony is that they are a product of their own system's programming. They look at being a teacher from the point of view of the 'E' quadrant rather than the 'B' or 'I' quadrant. Remember you can be anything you want to be in any of the quadrants . . . even a teacher.

We Can Be Anything We Want

Most of us have the potential to be successful in all of the quadrants. It all depends on how determined we are to be successful. As my rich dad said, 'Passion builds businesses. Not fear.'

The problem of changing quadrants is often found in our past conditioning. Many of us came from families where the emotion of fear was used as a prime motivator to get us to think and act in a certain way. For example:

'Did you do your homework? If you don't do your homework, you'll flunk out of school and all your friends will laugh at you.'

'If you keep making faces, your face will get stuck in that position.'

And the classic, 'If you don't get good grades, you won't get a safe, secure job with benefits.'

Well, today many people have gotten good grades, but there are fewer safe, secure jobs and even fewer with benefits, like retirement plans. So many people, even those with good grades, need to 'mind their own business' and not just look for a job where they will mind someone else's business.

It's Risky On The Left Side

I know many friends who still seek security in a job or a position. Ironically, the march of technology continues moving at an even faster pace. To keep up in the job market, each person will need to constantly be trained in the latest technology. If you're going to be re-educated anyway, why not spend some time educating yourself on the skills needed for the right side of the *Quadrant?* If people could see what I see when I travel the world, they would not be looking for more security. Security is a myth. Learn something new and take on this brave new world. Don't hide from it.

It is also risky for self-employed people, in my opinion. If they get sick, injured or die, their income is directly impacted. As I get older, I meet more self-employed people my age who are physically, mentally and emotionally burned out from hard work. The more fatigue a person endures, the less secure they become, and the risk of them having an accident also goes up.

It Is More Secure On The Right Side

The irony is, life is actually more secure on the right side of the *Quadrant*. For example, if you have a secure system that produces more and more money with less and less work, then you really do not need a job, or need to worry about losing your job or need to live life below your means. Instead of living below your means, expand your means. To make more money, simply expand the system and hire more people.

People who are high-level investors are not concerned about the market going up or going down because their knowledge will allow them to make money either way. If there is a market crash and/or a depression in the next 30 years, many baby boomers will panic, and lose much of the money they had set aside for retirement. If that happens in their old age, instead of retiring, they will have to work for as long as they can.

As for fear of losing money, professional investors are people who risk little of their own money and yet still make the highest returns. It is the people who know little about investing who take the risks and earn the least in return. From my point of view, all the risk is on the left side of the *Quadrant*.

Why The Left Side Is Riskier

'If you cannot read numbers, then you must take someone else's opinion,' said rich dad. 'In the case of buying a house, your dad just blindly accepts your banker's opinion that his house is an asset.'

Both Mike and I noticed his emphasis on the word 'blindly.'

'Most people on the left side really do not need to be that good with financial numbers. But if you want to be successful on the right side of the *Quadrant*, then numbers become your eyes. Numbers allow you to see what most people cannot see,' rich dad went on.

'You mean like Superman's X-ray vision,' said Mike.

Rich dad chuckled and nodded. 'Exactly,' he said. 'The ability to read numbers, financial systems and business systems gives you vision that mere mortals do not have.' Even he laughed at that silliness. 'Having financial vision lowers your risk. Being financially blind increases risk. But you only need that vision if you want to operate on the right side of the *Quadrant*. In fact, people on the left side think in words, and to be successful on the right, especially the 'I' quadrant, you must think in numbers . . . not words. It's really risky trying to be an investor while still thinking predominantly in words.'

'Are you saying that people on the left side of the *Quadrant* do not need to know about financial numbers?' I asked.

'For most of them, that is correct,' said rich dad. 'As long as they are content to operate strictly within the confines of being an 'E' or 'S,' then the numbers they learn in school are adequate. But if they want to survive on the right side, understanding financial numbers and systems becomes crucial. If you want to build a small business, you don't need to master numbers. But if you want build a large worldwide business, numbers become everything. Not words. That is why so many large companies are often run by bean counters.'

Rich dad continued his lesson: 'If you want to be successful on the right side, when it comes to money, you have got to know the difference between facts and opinions. You cannot blindly accept financial advice the way people on the left side do. You must know your numbers. You must know the facts. And numbers tell you the facts.'

Who Pays To Take The Risk?

'Besides the left side being risky, people on that side pay to take that risk,' said rich dad.'

'What did you mean by that last remark?' I asked. 'Doesn't everyone pay to take risks?

'No,' said rich dad. 'Not on the right side.'

'Are you trying to say that people on the left pay to take risks and the people on the right side get paid to take risks?'

'Exactly what I mean,' said rich dad, smiling. 'That is the biggest difference between the left side and the right side. That is why the left side is riskier than the right.

'Can you give me an example?' I asked.

'Sure,' said rich dad. 'If you buy shares of stock in a company, who takes the financial risk? You or the company?'

'I guess I do,' I said, still puzzled.

'And if I am a medical insurance company and I insure your health and take on your health risk, do I pay you?'

'No,' I said. 'If they insure my health, and they take that risk, I pay for it.'

'That's right,' said rich dad. 'I have yet to find an insurance company that will insure your health or accident risk and pay you for that privilege. But that is what people on the left side do.'

'It's kind of confusing,' said Mike. 'It still does not make sense.'

Rich dad smiled, 'Once you better understand the right side, you will begin to see the differences more clearly. Most people do not know there is a difference. They just assume everything is risky . . . and they pay for it. But as the years go on, and you become more comfortable with your experience and education on the right side of the *Quadrant*, your vision will improve and you will begin to see what people on the left side cannot see. And you will understand why seeking security to avoid risk is the riskiest thing you can do. You'll develop your own financial vision and not have to accept other people's opinions simply because they have a job title of banker, or stockbroker, or accountant, or whatever. You'll be able to see for yourself, and know the difference between financial facts and financial opinions.'

It was a good day. In fact, it was one of the better lessons I could remember. It was great because it began to open my mind to things my eyes could not see.

Numbers Reduce Risk

Without those simple lessons from my rich dad, I doubt if I could have taken my passion and built the educational system of my dreams. Without his insistence on financial literacy and accuracy,

I know I could not have invested as wisely, with so little of my own money and earned such high returns. I always remembered the bigger the project and the faster you want to succeed, the more you need to be accurate. If you want to get rich slowly, or just work all your life and let someone else manage your money, then you do not need to be as accurate. The faster you want to get rich, the more accurate with numbers you must be.

The good news is that due to advances in technology and new products, it is much easier today to learn the necessary skills for building your own system and quickly developing your financial literacy.

You Can Go Fast . . . But Don't Take Shortcuts

'To reduce your taxes, buy a bigger house and get deeper into debt so you can get a tax write-off.'

'Your home should be your largest investment.'

'You'd better buy now because the prices always go up.'

'Get rich slowly.'

'Live below your means.'

If you put in the time to study and learn about the subjects required on the right side of the *Quadrant*, such statements won't make much sense. It might make sense to someone on the left side of the *Quadrant*, but not to someone on the right side. You can do anything you like, go as fast as you like, make as much money as you like, but you have to pay the price. You can go quickly, but remember, there are no shortcuts.

This book is not about answers. This book is about looking at financial challenges and objectives from a different point of view. It's not that one point of view is better than another; it's simply smarter to have more than one point of view.

In reading the following chapters, you may begin looking at finances, business and life from a different point of view.

CHAPTER EIGHT

How Do I Get Rich?

When I am asked, 'Where did I learn my formula for getting rich?' I reply, 'Playing the game of *Monopoly* as a kid.'

Some people think I am kidding, and others wait for the punch line, expecting a joke. Yet, it is not meant as a joke, and I am not kidding. The formula for getting rich in *Monopoly* is simple, and it works in real life as well as in the game.

Four Green Houses . . . One Red Hotel

You may recall that the secret to wealth when playing *Monopoly* is simply to buy four green houses and then trade them in to buy a large red hotel. That is all it takes, and that is the same investment formula for wealth my wife and I used.

When the real estate market was really bad, we bought as many small houses as we could, with the limited money we had. When the market improved, we traded in the four green houses and bought a large red hotel. We never have to work because the cash flow from our large red hotel, apartment houses and mini storages pays for our lifestyle.

It Works For Hamburgers Also

Or if you do not like real estate, all you have to do is make hamburgers, build a business around that hamburger, and franchise it. Within a few years, the increasing cash flow will provide you with more money than you can spend.

In reality, that is how simple the path to extraordinary wealth can be. In other words, in this high-tech world, the principles of great wealth remain simple and low tech. I would say that it's merely common sense. But unfortunately, when it comes to the subject of money, common sense is uncommon.

For example, it makes no sense to me to give people a tax break to lose money and spend their lives in debt. Or to call your home an asset when it really is a liability that drains cash from you every day. Or to have a national government that spends more money than it collects in taxes. Or to send a child to school to study in the hope of getting a job, but not teach that child anything about money.

It Is Easy To Do What Rich People Do

Doing what rich people do is easy. One of the reasons there are so many wealthy people who did not do well in school is because the 'to do' part of becoming wealthy is simple. You do not have to go to school to become rich. The 'to do' part of becoming rich is definitely not rocket science.

There is a classic book I recommend you read: *Think and Grow Rich* by Napolean Hill. I read this book as a youngster, and it greatly influenced the direction of my life. In fact, it was my rich dad who first recommended I read this book and others like it.

There is a good reason why it's titled *Think and Grow Rich* and not Work Hard and Grow Rich or Get a Job and Grow Rich. The fact is, people who work the hardest do not wind up rich. If you want to be rich, you need to 'think.' Think independently rather than go along with the crowd. In my opinion, one great asset of the rich is they think differently from everyone else. If you do what everyone else does, you'll wind up having what everyone else has. And for most people, what they have is years of hard work, unfair taxes and a lifetime of debt.

When someone asks me, 'What do I have to do to move from the left side of the *Quadrant* to the right side?' my response is, 'It's not what you have to "do" that needs to change. It's first how you "think" that needs to change. In other words, it's who you have to "be" in order to "do" what needs to be done.'

Do you want to be the kind of person who thinks buying four green houses and turning them in for one red hotel is easy? Or do you want to be the kind of person who thinks buying four green houses and turning them in for one red hotel is hard?

Years ago I was in this class on goal setting. It was the mid-1970s, and I really could not believe I was spending $150 and a beautiful Saturday and Sunday to learn how to set goals. I would rather have been surfing. Instead, here I was paying someone to teach me how to set goals. I nearly backed out several times, but what I learned from that class has helped me achieve what I want in life.

The instructor put up on the board these three words.

BE – DO – HAVE

She then said, 'Goals are the "have" part of these three words. Goals such as to have a nice body, or to have the perfect relationship, or to have millions of dollars, or to have great health, or to have fame. Once most people figure out what they want to have, their goal, they begin listing what they have "to do." That is why most people have "To Do" lists. They set their goal and then begin "doing."'

She first used the goal of the perfect body. 'What most people do when they want a perfect body is go on a diet, and then go to the gym. This lasts for a few weeks and then most are back to the old diet of French fries and pizza, and instead of going to the gym, they watch baseball on TV. This is an example of "doing" instead of "being."'

'It's not the diet that counts; it's who you have to be to follow the diet that counts. Yet, every year millions of people look for the perfect diet to follow in order to become thin. They focus on what they have to do, rather than who they have to be. A diet will not help if your thoughts do not change.'

She used golf as another example: 'Many people buy a new set of golf clubs in hopes that they can improve their game, instead of starting with the attitude, mind-set and beliefs of a professional golfer. A lousy golfer with a new set of golf clubs is still a lousy golfer.'

Then, she discussed investments: 'Many people think that buying stocks or mutual funds will make them rich. Well, simply buying stocks, mutual funds, real estate and bonds will not make you rich. Just doing what professional investors do does not guarantee financial success. A person who has a loser mentality will always lose no matter what stock, bond, real estate or mutual fund they buy.'

Next, she used an example of finding the perfect romantic partner: 'So many people go to bars or to work or to their church looking for the perfect person, the person of their dreams. That is what they "do". What they "do" is go and look for the "right person" instead of work on "being the right person."'

Here's one of her examples about relationships: 'In marriage, many people try to change the other person so they can have a better marriage. Instead of trying to change the other person, which often leads to fights, it is better to change yourself first,' she said. 'Don't work on the other person; work on your thoughts about that other person.'

As she was talking about relationships, my mind drifted to the many people I had met over the years who were out to 'change the world' but were not getting anywhere. They wanted to change everyone else, but not change themselves.

For her example of money, she said, 'And when it comes to money, many people try "to do" what the rich do and "to have" what the rich have. So they go out and buy a house that looks rich, a car that looks rich, and send their kids to the schools where the rich send their kids. All this does is cause these people "to do" by working harder and "to have" more debt, which causes them to work even harder . . . which is not what the truly rich do.'

I was nodding my head in the back of the room in agreement. My rich dad did not use these same words to explain things, but he did often say to me, 'People think that working hard for money, and then buying things that make them look rich, will make them rich. In most cases it doesn't. It only makes them more tired. They call it "Keeping up with the Joneses," and if you notice, the Joneses are exhausted.'

During that weekend class, much of what my rich dad had been telling me began to make more sense. For years he lived modestly. Instead of working hard to pay bills, he worked hard to acquire assets. If you saw him on the street, he looked like everyone else. He drove a pickup truck, not an expensive car. Then one day, when he was in his late 30s, he emerged as a financial power-house. People took notice when he suddenly bought one of the prime pieces of real estate in Hawaii. After his name hit the paper, it was then people realized that this quiet unpretentious man owned many other businesses, lots of prime real estate, and when he spoke, his bankers listened. Few people ever saw the modest house he lived in. After he was flush with cash and cash flow from his assets, he then bought a new large house for his family. He did not take out a loan. He paid cash.

After that weekend class on goal setting, I realized that many people tried 'doing' what they thought the rich did and tried 'having' what the rich had. They often would buy big houses and invest in the stock market because that is what they thought the

175

rich did. Yet, what my rich dad was trying to tell me was if they still thought and had the beliefs and ideas of a poor person or middle-class person, and then did what the rich did, they would still wind up having what the poor and middle class have. 'Be-Do-Have' began to make sense.

The Cashflow Quadrant Is About Being . . . Not Doing

Moving from the left side of the *Quadrant* to the right side of the *Quadrant* is not so much about 'doing' but more about 'being.'

It is not so much what the 'B' or 'I' does that makes the difference; it is more how they 'think.' Who they are at their core 'being.'

The good news is that it does not cost much money to change your thinking. In fact, it can be done for free. The bad news is that sometimes it's hard to change some deep core thoughts about money that are handed down from generation to generation, or thoughts that you learned from friends, from work and from school. Yet, it can be done. And this is what this book is primarily about. It's not so much a 'How-to book' on 'What to do' to become financially free. This book is not about what stocks to buy, or what mutual fund is safest. This book is primarily about strengthening your thoughts (being), so that you can take the action (doing) that will enable you to become financially free (having).

Security Is The Issue For 'E's'

As a generalization, people who seek out the 'E' quadrant, when it comes to money, often greatly value security. For them, it is often true that money is not as important as security. They may take great risks in other areas of their lives, such as sport parachuting, but not when it comes to money.

Perfectionism Is The Issue For 'S's'

Again, this is a generalization . . . yet what I have observed among people who are currently in the 'S' quadrant, but are trying to switch from the left quadrant to right quadrant, is the 'Do it yourself' mentality. They like to 'Do it themselves' because they often have a great need to make sure things are done 'right.' And since they have a hard time finding someone else to do it 'right,' they do it on their own.

For many 'S's,' the real issue is 'control.' They need to be in control. They hate making mistakes. What they hate even more is someone else making mistakes and making them look bad. That is what makes them excellent 'S's' and the reason you hire them to do certain tasks for you. You want your dentist to be a perfectionist. You want your attorney to be a perfectionist. You want your brain surgeon to be a perfectionist. You want your architect to be a perfectionist. That is what you pay them for. That is their strength. It is also their weakness.

Emotional Intelligence

A big part of being a human being is being human. And being human means having emotions. All of us have the same emotions.

We all feel fear, sadness, anger, love, hate, disappointment, joy, happiness and other emotions. What makes us individuals is how we each handle those emotions.

When it comes to risking money, we all experience fear . . . even the rich. The difference is how we handle that fear. For many people, that emotion of fear generates the thought, 'Play it safe. Don't take risks.'

For others, especially those on the right side, fear of losing money may have them think this thought: 'Play it smart. Learn to manage risk.'

Same emotion, different thought . . . different being . . . different doing . . . different having.

The Fear Of Losing Money

In my opinion, the greatest cause of human financial struggle is the fear of losing money. And because of this fear, people often operate too safely, or with too much personal control, or they just give their money to someone they think is an expert and hope and pray that money will be there when they need it.

If fear keeps you prisoner in one of the financial quadrants, I recommend you read *Emotional Intelligence*, by Daniel Goleman. In his book, Goleman explains the age-old puzzle of why people who do well academically in school do not always do well financially in the real world. His answer is that Emotional IQ is more powerful than Academic IQ. That is why people who take risks, make mistakes and recover often do better than people who learned not to make mistakes because they were afraid of risk. Too many people leave school with passing grades, yet are not emotionally prepared to take risks . . . especially financial risks. The reason so many teachers are not rich is because they operate in a 'punish people who make mistakes environment,' and they themselves are often people who are emotionally afraid of making mistakes. Instead, to be financially free, we need to learn how to make mistakes and manage risk.

If people spend their life terrified of losing money, afraid of doing things differently from what the crowd does, then getting rich is almost impossible, even if it's as simple as buying four green houses and trading them in for one large red hotel.

Emotional IQ Is Stronger

After reading Goleman's book, I came to realize that Financial IQ is 90 percent Emotional IQ and only 10 percent technical information about finance or money. Goleman quotes 16th century humanist Erasmus of Rotterdam, who wrote a satirical vein of the perennial tension between reason and emotion. In his writing, he uses the ratio of 24:1 in comparing the power of the emotional brain to the rational brain. In other words, when emotions are in high gear, emotions are 24 times stronger than the rational mind. Now I do not know if the ratio is valid, but it does have some usefulness as a reference to the power of emotional thinking vs. rational thinking.

24 : 1

Emotional Brain : Rational Brain

All of us, if we are human, have experienced events in our lives when our emotions overtook our rational thoughts. I am certain most of us have:

1. Said something out of anger that we later wish we had not said.
2. Been attracted to someone we knew was not good for us . . . but still went out with them or, worse, married them.
3. Have cried, or seen someone cry uncontrollably, because of the loss of a loved one.
4. Did something intentionally to hurt someone we love because we were hurt.

5. Had our heart broken and not gotten over it for a long time.

Those are just a few examples of emotions being stronger than rational thought.

There are times when emotions are more than 24:1, and these are often called:

1. Addictions, such as compulsive eating, smoking, sex, shopping, drugs.
2. Phobias, such as fear of snakes, heights, tight spaces, the dark, strangers.

These and other behaviors are often 100 percent emotionally driven. There is little power that rational thought has over the emotional thought when something as strong as addictions and phobias are involved.

Snakes Phobia

When I was in flight school, I had a friend who had a phobia about snakes. During a class on how to survive in the wild after being shot down, the teacher brought out a harmless garden snake to show us how to eat it. My friend, a grown man, jumped up, screamed and ran out of the room. He could not control himself. Not only was his phobia of snakes strong, but the idea of eating a snake was just too much for his emotions to bear.

Money Phobia

When it comes to risking money, I have seen people do the same thing. Instead of finding out about the investment, they also jump up, scream and run out of the room.

When it comes to the subject of money, there are many deep emotional phobias . . . too many to list. I have them. You have them. We all have them. Why? Because like it or not, money is an emotional subject. And because it's an emotional subject, most people cannot think logically about money. If you don't think money is emotional, just watch the stock market. In most markets, there is no logic . . . only the emotions of greed and fear. Or just watch people climb into a new car and have them smell the leather interior. All the salesperson has to do is whisper these magic words in their ear, 'Low down, easy monthly payments,' and all logic goes out the window.

Emotional Thoughts Sound Logical

The problem with core emotional thoughts is that they sound logical. To someone in the 'E' quadrant, when the emotion of fear is present, the logical thought is: 'Play it safe, don't take risks.' To someone in the 'I' quadrant, however, this thought does not sound logical.

For people in the 'S' quadrant, when the issue of trusting other people to do a good job comes up, their logical thought may go like this: 'I'll just do it myself.'

That is a reason why so many 'S' type businesses are often family businesses. There is a greater sense of trust. For them, 'Blood is definitely thicker than water.'

So different quadrants . . . different logic . . . different thoughts . . . different actions . . . different haves . . . same emotions. Therefore, emotions make us human beings, and recognizing that we have emotions is a large part of being human.

What determines what we do is how we individually respond to those emotions.

I Don't Feel Like It

One way to know if you're thinking emotionally and not rationally is when you use the word 'feel' in conversation. For example, many people who are run by their emotions or their feelings will say things like: 'I don't feel like exercising today.' Logically they know they should exercise.

Many people who struggle financially are not able to control how they feel, or they let their feelings dictate their thoughts. I hear them say:

'I don't feel like learning about investing. It's too much trouble.'

'Investing doesn't feel right for me.'

'I don't feel like telling my friends about my business.'

'I hate the feeling of being rejected.'

Parent-Child-Adult

Those are thoughts generated from emotions, more than rationality. In pop psychology, it's the battle between the parent and child. The parent usually speaks in 'should's.' For example, a parent might say, 'You should be doing your homework,' while the child speaks in 'feeling.' In response to homework, a child would say, 'But I don't feel like doing it.'

Financially, the parent in you would say silently, 'You should save more money.' But the child in you would reply, 'But I really feel like taking a vacation. I'll just put the vacation on my credit card.'

When Are You An Adult?

In going from left quadrant to right quadrant, we need to be adults. We all need to grow up financially. Instead of being parent or child, we need to look at money, work, and investing as adults. And what being an adult means is knowing what you have to do and doing it, even though you may not feel like doing it.

Conversations Within You

For people contemplating making the crossing from one quadrant to another, an important part of the process is to be aware of your internal dialogue . . . or conversations within you. Always remember the importance of the book *Think and Grow Rich*. A significant part of the process is to be constantly vigilant regarding your silent thoughts, your internal dialogue, and always remember that what sounds logical in one quadrant does not make sense in another quadrant. The process of going from job or financial security to financial freedom is primarily a process of changing your thinking. It is a process of doing your best to know which thoughts are emotion-based and which thoughts are logic-based. If you can keep your emotions in check and go for what you know to be logical, you have a good chance of making the journey. No matter what anyone is saying to you from the outside, the most important conversation is the one you are having with yourself on the inside.

When Kim and I were temporarily homeless and financially unstable, our emotions were out of control. Many times, what sounded logical was pure emotions talking. Our emotions were saying the same thing our friends were saying: 'Play it safe. Just get a safe, secure job and enjoy life.'

Yet, logically, we both agreed that freedom made more sense to us than security. In going for financial freedom, we knew we could find a sense of security that job security could never give us. That made sense to us. The only things in our way were our emotionally driven thoughts. Thoughts that sounded logical but in the long term made no sense. The good news is that once we made it across, the old thoughts stopped screaming and the new thoughts we desired became our reality . . . the thoughts of the 'B' and 'I' quadrants.

Today, I understand the emotions when a person says:

'I can't take risks. I have a family to think about. I must have a secure job.'

Or 'It takes money to make money. That is why I can't invest.'

Or 'I'll do it on my own.'

I feel their thoughts, for I have had those thoughts myself. But looking across the *Quadrant* and having achieved financial freedom from the 'B' and 'I' quadrants, I can faithfully say that having financial freedom is a much more peaceful and secure way of thinking.

Differences Between 'E' And 'B'

Core emotional values cause different points of view. The struggle in communication between owners of a business and the employees of a business is often caused by differences in emotional values. There has always been a struggle between the 'E' and the 'B' because one wants more pay and the other wants more work. That is why we often hear, 'I'm overworked and underpaid.'

And from the other side we often hear, 'What can we do to motivate them to work harder and be more loyal without paying them any more?'

Differences Between 'B' And 'I'

Another is the constant tension between business operators and the investors in that business, often called the shareholders, the 'B' and the 'I.' One wants more money to operate with and the other wants greater dividends.

A conversation at a shareholders meeting may sound like this:

Company managers: 'We need a private jet so our executives can get to their meetings faster.'

Investors: 'We need fewer executives. Then, we won't need a private jet.'

Differences Between 'S' And 'B'

In business transactions, I have often seen a bright 'S,' such as an attorney, put a multimillion-dollar deal together for a 'B', business owner, and when the transaction is completed, the attorney becomes silently disturbed because the 'B' makes millions and the 'S' earns an hourly wage.

Their words may sound like this:

Attorney: 'We did all the work, and he made all the money.'

The 'B': 'How many hours did those guys bill us for? We could have bought the whole law firm for what they charged us.'

Differences Between 'E' And 'I'

Another example is a bank manager who gives an investor a loan to buy some real estate. The investor makes hundreds of thousands of dollars, tax free, and the banker gets a paycheck that is taxed heavily. That would be an example of an 'E' dealing with an 'I' that often causes a mild emotional reaction.

The 'E' might say: 'I give that guy a loan, and he doesn't even say "Thank you." I don't think he knows how hard we worked for him.'

The 'I' might say: 'Boy, those guys are picky. Look at all this useless paperwork we have to do just to get a lousy loan.'

Emotionally Disturbed Marriage

The most emotionally disturbed marriage I ever witnessed was a couple where the wife was a hard core 'E' who believed in job and financial security. The husband, on the other hand, fancied himself as a high-flying 'I.' He thought he was a future Warren Buffet, but in reality he was an 'S,' a commission-only salesman by profession, but he was a chronic gambler at heart. He was always looking for the investment that would help him 'Get rich quick.' He was all ears for any new stock offering, or off-shore investment scheme that promised ultra-high returns, or a real estate deal he could take an option on. This couple is still together, yet I really do not know why. Each drives the other nuts. One person thrives on risk; the other hates risk. Different quadrants, different core values.

If You Are Married Or In A Primary Relationship

If you are married or in a primary relationship, circle the quadrant you generate the majority of your income from and then circle the quadrant your spouse or partner generates income from.

The reason I ask you to do this is because the discussion between partners is often difficult if one partner does not understand where the other is coming from.

The Battle Between The Rich And The Educated

There is another unspoken battlefield I have noticed, and that is the differences in points of view between the educated and the rich.

In my years of researching the differences between the different quadrants, I have often heard bankers, attorneys, accountants and others like them grumble silently that they are the educated ones, and it's often the so-called less-educated person who makes the 'big bucks.' This is what I label the battle between the educated and the rich, which is more often the difference between people on the left side of the *Quadrant* and people on the right side of the *Quadrant* . . . or the 'E-S's' vs. the 'B-I's.' It's not that people in the 'B' and 'I' quadrant are uneducated . . . because many are highly educated; it's just that many 'B's' and 'I's' were not academic whiz kids in school . . . and were not trained in graduate schools like attorneys, accountants and MBAs were.

For those of you who read my book *Rich Dad Poor Dad*, you know it is about the struggle between the educated and the rich. My highly educated but poor dad took great pride in the fact that he had done years of advanced studies in prestigious schools such as Stanford University and The University of Chicago. My rich dad was a man who dropped out of school to run his family's business when his father died . . . so he never finished high school, yet he acquired tremendous wealth.

As I grew older and seemed to be more influenced by my rich but uneducated dad, my educated dad was occasionally defensive of his station in life. One day, when I was about 16 years of age, my educated dad blurted out,

'I have advanced degrees from prestigious schools. What does your friend's dad have?'

I paused and replied quietly, 'Money and free time.'

More Than A Mental Change

As stated earlier, to find success in the 'B' or 'I' quadrant requires more than simply academic or technical knowledge. It often requires a change in core emotional thinking, feelings, beliefs and attitude. Remember the

BE – DO – HAVE.

What the rich do is relatively simple. It's the 'Be' that is different. The difference is found in their thoughts and, more specifically, their internal dialogue with themselves. That is why my rich dad forbade me from saying:

'I can't afford it.'

'I can't do that.'

'Play it safe.'

'Don't lose money.'

'What if you fail and never recover?'

He forbade me from saying those words because he truly believed that words are the most powerful tools available to humans. What a person says and thinks becomes real.

He often quoted from the Bible, although he was not that religious: 'And the word became flesh and dwelt amongst us.'

Rich dad firmly believed that what we said to ourselves, at our core, became our reality. That is why I suspect that for people who struggle financially, their emotions often do the talking and run their lives. Until a person learns to overcome those emotionally driven thoughts, their words do become flesh. Words such as:

'I'll never be rich.'

'That idea will never work.'

'It's too expensive for me.'

If they are emotionally based thoughts, they are powerful. The good news is that they can be changed with support of new friends, new ideas and a little time.

People who are not able to control their fear of losing should never invest on their own. They are best served by turning that job over to a professional and not interfering with them.

As an interesting note, I have met many professional people who are fearless when investing other people's money and able to make lots of money. But when it comes to investing or risking their own money, their fear of losing becomes too strong and they ultimately lose. Their emotions do the thinking rather than their logic.

I have also met people who can invest their money and win constantly, but lose their calm when someone asks them to invest money for them.

The making and losing of money is an emotional subject. So my rich dad gave me the secret to handling these emotions. Rich dad always said, 'To be successful as an investor or a business owner, you have to be emotionally neutral to winning and losing. Winning and losing are just part of the game.'

Quitting my Secure Job

My friend Mike had a system that belonged to him. His father had built it. I did not have that good fortune. I knew that someday I was going to have to leave the comfort and security of the nest, and begin to build my own.

In 1978, I resigned from my full-time secure job with Xerox, and took the hard step forward with no safety net. The noise in my head was loud from my fear and doubt. I was nearly paralyzed with fear as I signed my letter of resignation, collected my last paycheck, and walked out the door. I had an orchestra of self-damaging thoughts and feelings playing inside me. I was 'bad-mouthing' myself so loudly and with such conviction that I could not hear anything else. It's a good thing, because so many of the people I worked with were saying, 'He'll be back. He'll never make it.'

The problem was, I was saying the same thing to myself. Those emotional words of self-doubt haunted me for years until my wife and I were successful in both the 'B' and 'I' quadrants. Today, I still hear those words; they just have less authority. In the process of putting up with my own self-doubt, I learned to create other words, words of personal encouragement, statements such as:

'Keep calm, think clearly, keep an open mind, keep going, ask someone who has gone before you for some guidance, trust, and keep the faith in a higher power wanting the best for you.'

I learned to create these words of encouragement internally, even though there was a part of me that was frightened and afraid.'

I knew that I had little chance of success my first time out. Yet, the positive human emotions, emotions such as trust, faith, courage and good friends moved me forward. I knew that I had to take risks. I knew that risk led to mistakes, and mistakes led to wisdom and knowledge, both of which I lacked. For me, failure would have been to let fear win, so I was willing to move forward with little in guarantees. My rich dad had instilled in me the idea that 'failure is part of the process of success.'

Internal Journey

The journey from one quadrant to the next is an internal journey. It is a journey from one set of core beliefs and technical skills to a new set of core beliefs and a new set of technical skills. The process is much like learning to ride a bicycle. At first you fall down many times. Often it's frustrating and embarrassing, especially if your friends are watching. But after a while, the falling stops and riding becomes automatic. If you fall down again, it's not that big of a deal because, internally, you now know that you can get up and ride again. The process is the same when going from an emotional mind-set of job security to the emotional mind-set of financial freedom. Once my wife and I made the crossing, we were less afraid of failing because we were confident in our ability to stand back up.

There are two statements that kept me going personally. One was my rich dad's words of advice, when I was on the brink of quitting and turning back: 'You can always quit . . . so why quit now?'

That statement kept my spirits higher and emotions calm. That statement reminded me that I was halfway across . . . so why turn back because the distance going home was just as far as going for the quadrant on the other side. It would be like Columbus quitting and turning back halfway across the Atlantic. Either way, the distance was the same.

And a word of caution: Intelligence is also knowing when to quit. Too often I meet people who are so stubborn, they keep going forward on a project that has no chance of success. The problem of knowing when to quit or when to keep going is an age-old problem with anyone who takes risks. One way to manage this problem of 'to keep going or quit' is to find mentors who have already successfully made the crossing before, and seek their advice. Such a person, who is already on the other side, can best guide you. But be careful of advice from someone who has only read books about the crossing and gets paid to lecture on the subject.

The other statement that often kept me going was:

'Giants often trip and fall.

But worms don't, because

All they do is dig and crawl.'

The main reason so many people struggle financially is not because they lack a good education, or are not hard working. It's because they're afraid of losing. If the fear of losing stops them, they've already lost.

Losers Cut Their Winners And Ride Their Losers

Fear of 'being' a loser affects what people 'do' in strange ways. I have seen people who bought a stock at $20, sell their shares when they reached $30 because they're so afraid of losing what they've gained, only to have the stock go to $100, split and go up to $100 again.

That same person, having bought a stock at $20, will watch it go down to, say, $3 and still hang on, hoping the price will come back up . . . and they may hang on to that $3 stock for 20 years. This is an example of a person 'being' so afraid of losing, or admitting they lost, that they wind up losing.

Winners Cut Their Losers And Ride Their Winners

Winners 'do' things almost exactly the opposite. Often, the moment they know they took a losing position, i.e. their stock price starts to go down instead of up, they will sell immediately and take their losses. Most are not ashamed to say they took a loss, for a winner knows that losing is part of the process of winning.

When they find a winner, they will ride it up as far as it can go. The moment they know the free ride is over and the price has peaked, they cut and sell.

The key to being a great investor is to be neutral to winning and losing. Then, you don't have emotionally driven thoughts such as fear and greed doing your thinking for you.

Losers Do The Same Things In Life

People who are afraid of losing do the same things in real life. We all know of:

1. People who stay in marriages where there is no longer any love.
2. People who stay at dead-end jobs.
3. People who hang on to old clothes and 'stuff' they will never use.
4. People who stay in towns where they have no future.
5. People who stay friends with people who hold them back.

Emotional Intelligence Can Be Controlled

Financial intelligence is closely linked to emotional intelligence. In my opinion, most people suffer financially because their emotions are in control of their thoughts. We as human BE-ings, all have the same emotions. What determines the differences in what we 'DO' and what we 'HAVE' in life is primarily how we handle those emotions.

For example, the emotion of fear can cause some of us to be cowards. The same emotion of fear can cause others to become courageous. Unfortunately, when it comes to the subject of money, most people in our society are conditioned to be financial cowards. When the fear of losing money comes up, most people's minds automatically start chanting these words:

1. 'Security,' rather than 'freedom.'
2. 'Avoid risk,' rather than 'learn to manage risk.'
3. 'Play it safe,' rather than 'play it smart.'
4. 'I can't afford it,' rather than 'how can I afford it?'
5. 'It's too expensive,' rather than 'what is it worth, long term?'
6. 'Diversify,' rather than 'focus.'
7. 'What will my friends think?' rather than 'what do I think?'

The Wisdom Of Risk

There is a science to taking risks, especially financial risks. One of the best books I have read on the subject of money and risk management is *Trading for a Living*, by Dr. Alexander Elder.

Although it was written for people who trade stocks and options professionally, the wisdom of risk and risk management applies to all areas of money, money management, personal psychology and investing. One of the reasons many successful 'B's' are not always as successful as 'I's' is because they do not fully understand the psychology behind purely risking money. While 'B's' understand risk when it involves business systems and people, that knowledge does not always translate into the systems of money making money.

It's Emotional More Than Technical

In summary, moving from quadrants on the left to quadrants on the right is more emotional than technical. If people are not able to control their emotional thoughts, I would not recommend the journey.

The reason things look so risky on the right side of the *Quadrant* to people on the left side is because the emotion of fear is often affecting their thinking. People on the left side think 'play it safe' is a logical thought. It isn't. It's an emotional thought. And it's the emotional thoughts that keep people stuck to one quadrant or the other.

What people 'DO' on the right side of the equation is not that hard. I am sincere when I say that it is as easy as buying four green houses for low prices, waiting until the market improves, selling them and then buying a big red hotel.

Life really is a game of *Monopoly* for people on the right side of the quadrant. Sure, there is winning and losing, but that is part of the game. Winning and losing is a part of life. To be successful on the right side of the *Quadrant* is to 'BE' a person who loves the game. Tiger Woods loses more than he wins, yet he still loves the game. Donald Trump went broke and battled back. He didn't quit because he lost. Losing only made him smarter and more determined. Many wealthy people went broke before they became rich. It's a part of the game.

If a person's emotions are thinking for them, those emotional thoughts often blind that person from seeing anything else. It is because of those knee-jerk emotional thoughts that people react, rather than think. It is those emotions that cause people from different quadrants to argue. The arguments are caused by people not having the same emotional points of view. It is that emotional reaction that blinds a person from seeing how easy, and often risk free, things are on the right side of the *Quadrant*. If a person cannot control their emotional thoughts, and many cannot, then they should not attempt to make the crossing.

I encourage all of you wanting to make the crossing to make sure you have a long-term positive support group with you and a mentor on the other side guiding you. To me, the struggle my wife and I went through was worth it. For us, the most important thing about crossing from the left side to the right side of the *Quadrant* is not what we had to 'do,' but who we became in the process. To me, that is priceless.

CHAPTER NINE

Be The Bank . . .
Not The Banker

I have focused on the 'BE' portion of the formula 'BE-DO-HAVE' because without the proper mind-set and attitude, you cannot be prepared for the great economic changes that are facing us today. By 'being' someone with the skills and mind-set of the right side of the *Quadrant*, you will be prepared to recognize opportunities that arise from these changes and be prepared to 'DO' what will result in your 'HAVING' financial success.

I remember a phone call I received from my rich dad in late 1986:

'Are you in the real estate market or the stock market?' he asked.

'Neither,' I replied. 'Everything I have is invested in building my business.'

'Good,' he said. 'Stay out of all markets. Keep building your business. Something big is about to happen.'

That year, the U.S. Congress passed the Tax Reform Act of 1986. In a swift 43 days, Congress took away many of the tax loopholes that people counted on to shelter their income. For people who were using those 'passive losses' from their income property as tax deductions, they suddenly still had their losses, but the government had taken away the tax deduction. All across

America, real estate prices began to plunge. Property prices began to slide, in some cases as much as a 70 percent. Suddenly, properties were worth far less than the amount of their mortgages. Panic swept the entire property market. Banks and savings and loans began to shake, many began to fail. People could not get their money out of the banks and then Wall Street crashed in October 1987. The world went into financial crisis.

Fundamentally, the Tax Reform Act of 1986 took away many of the tax loopholes that, on the left side of the *Quadrant*, high-income 'E's' and 'S's' depended on. Many of them had invested in real estate properties or limited partnerships in order to utilize these losses to offset their earnings from the 'E' and/or 'S' quadrants. And while the crash and recession did affect the people on the right side of the *Quadrant*, the 'B' and 'I' quadrants, many of their tax-avoidance mechanisms were left intact.

During this period, 'E's' learned a new word. That word was 'downsizing.' They soon realized that when a major layoff was announced, the share price of the stock of the company announcing the lay off went up. Sadly, most did not understand why. There were many 'S's' who were also struggling to cope with the recession, due to a decrease in business, higher insurance rates, as well as losses from the real estate and share markets. As a result, I feel that individuals primarily focused in the left side of the *Quadrant* were hurt and suffered the most financially as a direct result of the Tax Reform Act of 1986.

Transfer Of Wealth

While people on the left side were suffering, many people who operated on the 'B' and 'I' side of the *Quadrant* were getting rich, thanks to the government taking away from some people to give to others.

By changing the tax code, all the 'tax trick' reasons for investing were taken away from people who were simply buying real estate to lose money. Many were high-income employees, or professional people such as doctors, attorneys, accountants and small-business owners. Prior to this period, they had so much taxable income that their advisers told them to buy real estate to lose money, and then with any extra money, invest in the stock market. When the government took that loophole away with the Tax Reform Act . . . one of the most massive transfers of wealth began. In my opinion, much of the wealth was taken away from the 'E' and 'S' side of the *Quadrant* and handed to the 'B' and 'I' side for pennies on the dollar.

When the savings and loans, the organizations that issued the bad loans, failed, billions of dollars in deposits were at risk. The money had to be paid back. So who was left to pay back the billions of dollars lost in savings and real estate foreclosures? Well, the taxpayers of course. The very people who were already hurting enough as it was. And the taxpayers were stuck with a multibillion-dollar bill for this tax law change.

Some of you may also remember a governmental agency called the Resolution Trust Corporation, or the RTC as it was commonly known. The RTC was the agency responsible for taking the fore-closures from the real estate crash, and transferring them to people who knew how to handle them. For me and many of my friends, it was like a blessing from financial heaven.

Money, you'll recall, is seen with the mind . . . not the eyes. During this period of time, emotions ran high and visions were blurred. People saw what they were trained to see. Three things happened to the people on the left side of the *Quadrant*.

1. Panic was everywhere. When emotions are high, financial intelligence often disappears. Because people were so concerned about their jobs, the falling value of their property, the crash of the stock market, and the general slowdown of business, they failed to see the massive

197

opportunities right in front of them. Their emotional thoughts had blinded them. Instead of moving forward and beating the bushes, most people went into their caves and hid.

2. They lacked the technical skills required on the right side of the *Quadrant*. Just as a doctor must have technical skills developed from years of schooling and then from on-the-job training, someone in the 'B' quadrant and the 'I' quadrant must also possess highly specialized technical skills. Technical skills that include financial literacy, which is knowing the vocabulary, how to restructure debt, how to structure an offering, who your market is, how to raise capital, and other learnable skills.

   When the RTC said, 'We have a banker's box for sale, and in it is property that used to be worth $20 million . . . but you can have it today for $4 million,' most people on the left side of the *Quadrant* did not have a clue how to raise the $4 million to buy the gift from financial heaven or know how to recognize the good deals from the bad deals.

3. They lacked a cash machine. Most people during this period had to work harder just to survive. By operating as a 'B,' my business could expand with little physical effort on my part. By 1990, my business was up and running and growing. During this period, the business grew from a start-up to 11 offices worldwide. The more it expanded, the less physical work I had to do, and the more money came in. The system and the people in the system were working hard. With the extra money and free time, my wife and I were able to spend a lot of time looking at 'deals' . . . and there were many of them.

It Was The Best Of Times . . .
It Was The Worst Of Times

There is a saying that goes: 'It is not what happens in one's life that matters . . . but it is the meaning one puts on what happens that matters.'

The period from 1986 to 1996 was, for some people, the worst time of their lives. For others, it was the best of times. When I received that phone call from my rich dad in 1986, I recognized the fantastic opportunity that this economic change presented me. Even though I did not have a lot of extra cash at the time, I was able to create assets by utilizing my skills as a 'B' and an 'I.' Later in this chapter, I will describe in greater detail how I created assets that helped me become financially free.

One of the keys to a successful and happy life is to be flexible enough to respond appropriately to whatever change comes your way – to be able to respond and make a good thing out of anything. Unfortunately, most people have not been equipped to handle the fast-breaking economic changes that have happened and continue to happen. There is one thing that is a blessing with human beings: They are generally optimistic, and have the ability to forget. After about 10 to 12 years, they forget . . . and then things change again.

History Repeats Itself

Today, people have more or less forgotten about the Tax Reform Act of 1986. The 'E's' and 'S's' are working harder than ever. Why? Because their tax loopholes were taken away. As they have worked harder to get back what they lost, the economy has improved, their incomes have gone up, and their tax accountant has again started whispering the same old words of wisdom:

'Go buy a bigger house. Interest on your debt is your best tax deduction. And besides, your home is an asset, and it should be your largest investment.'

So they look at 'the easy monthly payments,' and they get sucked into a higher debt position.

The housing market is booming, people have more disposable income, and interest rates are low. People are buying bigger houses, their mood is euphoric, and they are pouring money into the stock market because they want to get rich quickly and they have realized they need to invest for retirement.

Again, in my opinion, a great transfer of wealth is about to happen. It may not happen this year, but it will happen. It will just not happen in exactly the same way. Something different will happen. This is why my rich dad had me read books on economic history. Economics change, but history repeats. It just does not read on the same set of circumstances.

Money continues to flow from the left side to the right side of the *Quadrant*. It always has. Many people are deeply in debt, yet they pour money into the biggest stock market boom in the history of the world. The people on the right side of the *Quadrant* will sell at the top of the market, just when the last cautious people on the left side overcome their fear and enter the market. Something newsworthy will happen, the market will crash, and when the dust settles, the investors will move back in. They will buy back what they just sold. Again, we will have another great transfer of wealth from the left side to the right side of the *Quadrant*.

It will take at least another 12 years for the emotional scars to heal of those who lose money . . . but the wounds will heal, just as another market is nearing its peak.

At about that time, people will begin quoting Yogi Berra, the great New York Yankees baseball player: 'It's deja vu all over again.'

Is It A Conspiracy?

Often I hear people, especially people on the left side of the *Quadrant*, say that there is some kind of global conspiracy, held together by a few ultra-rich families that control the banks.

These banking conspiracy theories have been around for years.

Is there a conspiracy? I do not know. Could there be a conspiracy? Anything is possible. I know there are powerful families who control massive sums of money. But does one group control the world? I don't think so.

I see it differently. I see it more or less as one group of people on one side of the *Quadrant* with one mind-set and another group of people on the other side of the *Quadrant* with a different mind-set. They're all playing this one big game of money, but each quadrant is playing from a different point of view and with a different set of rules.

The big problem is, the people on the left side are unable to see what the people on the right side are doing, but the people on the right side know what the people on the left are doing.

Witch Hunts

Many people on the left side of the *Quadrant*, instead of finding out what the people on the right side know that they do not, go on witch hunts. Only a few centuries ago, when there was a plague, or something had happened to a community, townspeople would go on a 'witch hunt.' They needed someone to blame for their plight. Until science invented the microscope and people could see what their naked eyes could not, which were germs, people blamed other people for their diseases. They burned witches at the stake to solve their problems. Little did they know that most of the disease was caused by people living in cities with poor garbage and sewage disposal. People had caused their own problems by using unsanitary conditions . . . not the 'witches'.

Well, witch hunts still go on today. Many people look for someone to blame for their financial plight. These people often want to blame the rich for their personal financial problems, rather than realize it is often their own lack of information about money that is a fundamental reason for their plight.

Heroes Become Villains

Every few years a new financial guru appears and seems to have the new magic formula for wealth. In the late 1970s, it was the Hunt brothers who tried to corner the silver market. The world applauded their genius. Almost overnight, they were hunted down as criminals because so many people lost money after they followed the brothers' advice. In the late 1980s, it was Michael Milken, the junkbond king. One day he was a financial genius, and right after the crash he was tracked down and sent to jail. The individuals change, but history repeats.

Today, we have new investment geniuses. They come across on television, their names are in the paper, they are the new celebrities. One of them is Alan Greenspan, the chairman of the Federal Reserve Board. Today, he is nearly a god. People think he is responsible for our wonderful economy. Warren Buffet is also touted as a near god. When he buys something, everybody rushes in and buys what he buys. And when Warren Buffet sells, prices crash. Bill Gates is also watched carefully. Money will follow him freely. If there is a major market correction in the near future, will today's financial heroes be tomorrow's hated? Only time will tell.

In every 'up' cycle of the economy, there are heroes, and in every 'down' cycle, there are villains. In reviewing history, they have often been the same people. People will always need witches to burn or conspiracies to blame for their own financial blindness. History will repeat itself . . . and again a great transfer of wealth will take place. And when it does, which side of the transfer will you be on? The left side or the right side?

In my opinion, people simply fail to realize that they are in this large global game . . . a virtual casino in the sky, but no one told them that they were an important player in the game. The game is 'Who Is Indebted To Whom?'

Being The Bank . . . Not The Banker

In my mid-20s, it dawned on me that the name of the game was to be the bank, but that didn't mean to get a job as a banker. My advanced education was about to begin. It was during this period that my rich dad had me look up words like 'mortgage,' 'real estate' and 'finance.' I was beginning to train my mind to see what my eyes could not.

He encouraged me to learn and understand the game, and then after I learned the game, I could do what I wanted with what I found. I decided to share my knowledge with anyone who was interested.

He also had me read books on the great leaders of capitalism. People such as John D. Rockefeller, J.P. Morgan, Henry Ford. One of the most important books I read was *The Worldly Philosophers*, by Robert Heilbroner. For people who want to operate on the 'B' and 'I' side, his book is a must read, for it traces the greatest economists of all time, starting with Adam Smith, who wrote *The Wealth of Nations*. It is fascinating to look into the minds of some of our most important philosophers, the economists. These people interpreted the evolution of modern capitalism over its brief history. In my opinion, if you want to be a leader on the right side of the *Quadrant*, a historical view of economic history is important to understanding both our history and future.

After *The Worldly Philosophers*, I recommend reading Paul Zane Pilzer's *Unlimited Wealth*, James Dale Davidson's *The Sovereign Individual*, Robert Prechter's *The Crest of the Wave*, and Harry Dent's *The Great Boom Ahead*. Heilbroner's book gives you insight into where we have come from economically, and the other authors give their views on where we are headed. Their contrasting viewpoints are important in allowing me to see what my eyes cannot . . . something called the future. By reading books like these, I have been able to gain insights into the ups and downs of cycles and trends of the economy. A common theme in all of these books is that one of the biggest changes of all is right around the corner.

How To Play The Bank

After the 1986 Tax Reform Act, there were opportunities every-where. Real estate, stocks and businesses were available for low prices. While it was devastating for many people on the left side of the *Quadrant*, it was wonderful for me because I could utilize my skills as a 'B' and 'I' to take advantage of the opportunities around me. Instead of being greedy and chasing everything that looked like a good deal, I decided to focus on real estate.

Why real estate? For these five simple reasons:

1. **Pricing.** The prices of real estate were so low that mort-gage payments were far lower than the fair market rent for most properties. These properties made great economic sense . . . which meant there was little risk. It was like going to a sale at a department store when everything was priced 50 percent off.

2. **Financing.** The banks would give me a loan on real estate, but not on stocks. Since I wanted to buy as much as I could while the market was depressed, I bought real estate so that what cash I had could be combined with financing through banks.

   For example: Let's say I had $10,000 in savings to invest. If I bought stocks, I could buy $10,000 worth of stocks. I could have gone on margin (when you buy on margin you put up only part of the total cost and the broker company lends you the remainder), but I was not financially strong enough to risk a downturn in the market.

With $10,000 in real estate, and a 90 percent loan, I could buy a $100,000 property.

If both markets went up 10 percent, I would make $1,000 in stocks, but $10,000 in real estate.

3. **Taxes.** If I made $1 million in profit from stocks, I would have to pay nearly 30 percent in capital gains tax on my profit. In real estate, however, the $1 million could be rolled tax free into the next real estate transaction. On top of that, I could depreciate the property for even greater tax advantages.

Important note: An investment must make economic sense before the tax benefit for me to invest in it. Any tax benefit only makes the investment more attractive.

4. **Cash flow.** Rents had not declined even though the real estate prices had declined. This put a lot of money into my pocket, paid for the mortgages, and most importantly allowed me to 'time' the market. Rents bought me time to wait until real estate prices went up again. When they did, I was able to sell. Although I carried large debt, it never hurt me because the rents were far greater than the cost of carrying the loan.

5. **An opportunity to become a bank.** Real estate allowed me to become a bank, something I had always wanted to do since 1974.

Be The Bank, Not A Banker

In *Rich Dad Poor Dad*, I wrote about how the rich create money and often play the role of banker. The following is a simple example that almost anyone can follow.

Let's say I find a house that is worth $100,000 and I get a

heck of a deal and only pay $80,000 for it (a $10,000 down payment plus a $70,000 mortgage I am responsible for.)

I then advertise that the house is available for sale for $100,000, which is its appraised price, and use these magic words in the ad: 'House for sale. Owner desperate. No bank qualifying. Low down payment, easy monthly payments.'

The phone rings like crazy. The house is sold on what is called a 'wrap' or a 'lease purchase contract,' depending on which country you're in. In simple terms, I sell the house for a $100,000 IOU. This is what the transaction looks like:

on my balance sheet

My Balance Sheet

Assets	Liabilities
$100,000 IOU	$70,000 Mortgage

on the buyer's balance sheet

Buyer's Balance Sheet

Assets	Liabilities
	$100,000 IOU

This transaction is then registered with a title and escrow office, which often handles the payments. If the person defaults on the $100,000, I simply foreclose and sell the property to the next person who wants a 'low down, easy monthly payment' home to live in. People line up for the opportunity to buy a home on these terms.

The net effect is that I have created $30,000 in my asset column for which I am paid interest, just like a bank gets paid interest for loans it makes.

I was beginning to be a bank, and I loved it. If you recall from the last chapter, rich dad said: 'Be careful when you take on debt. If you take on debt personally, make sure it's small. If you take on large debt, make sure someone else is paying for it.'

In the language of the right side of the *Quadrant*, I 'laid off' my risk, or 'hedged' my risk on to another buyer. That is the game in the world of finance.

This type of transaction is done all over the world. Yet, wherever I go, people come up to me and say those magic words, 'You can't do that here.'

What most small investors fail to realize is that many large commercial buildings are bought and sold exactly in the manner described above. Sometimes they go through a bank, but many times they do not.

It's Like Saving $30,000 Without Saving

If you remember from a previous chapter, I wrote about why the government did not give people a tax advantage for saving money. Well, I doubt if the banks ever will ask the government to do so because your savings are their liability. The U.S. has a low savings rate simply because banks do not want your money or need your savings to do well. So this example is a way of playing bank and increasing your savings without a great deal of effort. The cash flow from this $30,000 is reflected as follows:

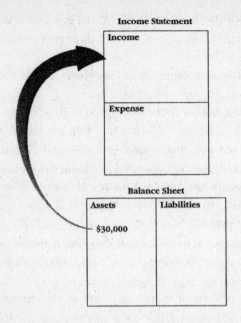

There are several interesting things about this diagram:

1. I determine the interest rate from my $30,000. Often it's 10 percent interest. Most banks don't pay you more than 5 percent on your savings today. So even if I did use my own $10,000 as a down payment, which I try not to do, the interest on it is often better than the bank would pay me.

2. It's like creating $20,000 ($30,000–$10,000 down payment) that did not exist before. Just like the bank does . . . it creates an asset and then charges interest on it.

3. This $20,000 was created tax free. For the average person in the 'E' quadrant, it would have taken nearly $40,000 of wages to be able to set aside $20,000. Income earned as an

employee is a 50–50 proposition, with the government taking its 50 percent before you ever see it through withholding.

4. All property taxes, maintenance and management fees are now the responsibility of the buyer, because I sold the property to the buyer.

5. And there is more. Many creative things can be done on the right side of the *Quadrant* to create money from nothing, just by playing the role of the bank.

A transaction like this may take a week to a month to put together. The question is how long would it take for most people to earn an additional $40,000 so they can save $20,000 after running the gauntlet of taxes and other expenses incurred to earn that money.

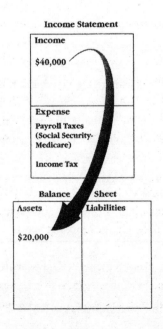

The Income Stream Is Then Sheltered

In *Rich Dad Poor Dad*, I briefly covered why the rich use corporations:

1. Asset protection. If you're rich, people tend to want to take what you have through litigation. It is called, 'Look for someone with deep pockets.' The rich often don't own anything in their own names. Their assets are held in trusts and corporations to protect them.

2. Income protection. By passing the income stream from assets through your own corporation, much of what is normally taken from you by the government can be sheltered.

The harsh reality: If you are an employee, the sequence goes like this.

EARN – TAXED – SPEND

As an employee, your earnings are taxed and taken through withholding even before you get your paycheck. So if an employee is paid $30,000 per year, by the time the government gets through with it, it's down to $15,000. With this $15,000 you must then pay your mortgage. (But at least you get a tax deduction for the interest paid on your mortgage . . . which is how the bank convinces you to buy a bigger house.)

If you pass your income stream through a corporate entity first, this is what the pattern would look like.

EARN – SPEND – TAXED

By passing the income stream from the $30,000 you invented first through a corporation, you can 'expense' much of the earnings before the government gets it. If you own the corporation, you make the rules . . . as long as it conforms with the tax code.

For example, if you make the rules, you can write into the bylaws of your company that child care is part of your employment package. The company may pay $400 per month for child care out of pre-tax dollars. If you pay for it with after-tax dollars, you have to effectively earn close to $800 to pay for that same child care with after-tax dollars. The list is long and the requirements are specific as to what an owner of a corporation can write off that an employee cannot. Even certain travel expenses can be written off with pre-tax dollars as long as you can document that you conducted business on the trip (eg. you hold a board meeting). Just make sure you follow the rules. Even retirement plans are different for owners and employees in many instances. Having said all of this, I want to stress that you must follow the regulations required to make these expenses deductible. I believe in taking advantage of the legal deductions allowed by the tax code but I do not recommend breaking the law.

Again, the key to being able to take advantage of some of these provisions is which quadrant you earn your income from. If all of your income is generated as an employee from a company that you do not own or control, there is little income or asset protection available to you.

That's why I recommend that if you are an employee, keep your job, but begin to spend time in the 'B' or 'I' quadrants. Your road to faster freedom is through those two quadrants. To feel more financially secure, the secret is to operate in more than one quadrant.

Free Land

A few years ago, my wife and I wanted some property away from the maddening crowds. We got the urge to own some acreage with tall oak trees with a stream running through it. We also wanted privacy.

We found a parcel with a price of $75,000 for 20 acres. The seller was willing to take 10 percent down and carry the balance at 10 percent interest. It was a fair transaction. The problem was it violated the rule on debt that my rich dad had taught me, which was: 'Be careful when you take on debt. If you take on debt personally, make sure it's small. If you take on large debt, make sure someone else pays for it.'

My wife and I passed on the $75,000 piece of land and went looking for a piece of land that made more sense. To me, $75,000 is a lot of debt because our cash flow would have looked like this:

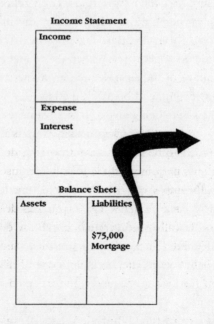

And remember my rich dad's rule:

'If you take on debt and risk, then you should be paid.'

Well, in this transaction, I would have taken on both the debt and the risk, and I was paying for it.

About a month later, we found a piece of land that was even more beautiful. It was 87 acres of tall oak trees with a stream, and it had a house on it, for $115,000. I offered the seller full price, if he would give me my terms . . . and he did. To make a long story short, we spent a few dollars fixing the house and sold the house and 30 acres for $215,000, using the same idea of 'low down, easy monthly payments,' all while keeping 57 acres for ourselves.

This is what the transaction looks like on my balance sheet.

Balance Sheet

Assets	Liabilities
$215,000	$115,000

The new owner was thrilled because it was a beautiful home and he was able to buy it for almost nothing down. As an aside, he also bought it through his company for use as a corporate retreat for his employees, which allowed him to depreciate the purchase price as a company asset as well as deduct the maintenance costs. This, all in addition to being able to deduct the interest payments. His interest payments more than paid for my interest payments. A few years later, he sold some of his company stock and paid off the loan to me, and I, in turn, paid off my loan. The debt was gone.

With the extra $100,000 profit I made, I was able to pay the taxes from the gain of the land and the house.

The net result was zero debt, a few dollars profit ($15,000

213

after taxes), and the 57 acres of gorgeous land. It was like getting paid for getting what you want.

Today, my balance sheet from that one transaction looks like this:

Balance Sheet

Assets	Liabilities
57 Acres Land $15,000 Cash	

The IPO

An initial public offering (IPO), or taking a private company public through a stock offering, is based on the same principles. While the words, the market and the players are different, there are basic underlying principles that remain the same. When my organization forms a company to take public, we often create a value out of thin air, even though we try to base it on an accurate opinion of the fair market value. We take the offering to the public market, and instead of this equity being sold to one person, it is sold to thousands of people as shares of a company.

The Value Of Experience

This is another reason I recommend people start in the 'B' quadrant before proceeding to the 'I' quadrant. Regardless of whether the investment is in real estate, a business, stocks or bonds, there is an underlying 'comprehensive business sense' that is essential to being a sound investor. Some people have this comprehensive sense, but many do not. Primarily because school trains us to be highly specialized . . . not comprehensively trained.

One more point, for those thinking about starting to move over to the 'B' or 'I' quadrants, I recommend starting small . . . and taking your time. Do bigger deals as your confidence grows and experience grows. Remember, the only difference between an $80,000 deal and an $800,000 deal is a zero. The process of going through a small deal is much the same as going through a much larger multimillion-dollar public offering. It's only a matter of more people, more zeros and more fun.

Once a person gains experience and a good reputation, it takes less and less money to create bigger and bigger investments. Many times it takes no money to make a lot of money. Why? Experience is valuable. As stated earlier, if you know how to make money with money, people and money will flock to you. Start small and take your time. Experience is more important than money.

It Is Simple And Easy

In theory, the numbers and transactions on the right side of the *Quadrant* are that simple, regardless of whether we're talking about stocks, bonds, real estate or businesses. To be financially well off simply means being able to think differently . . . to think from different quadrants and to have the courage to do things differently. To me, one of the hardest things a person who is new to this way of thinking has to go through is the countless number of people who will say to you: 'You can't do that.'

If you can overcome that kind of limited thinking, and seek out people who say to you, 'Yes, I know how to do that. I'd be happy to teach you,' your life will be easy.

The Laws

I started this chapter with the Tax Reform Act of 1986. While that was a significant rule change, it is not and will not be the last rule change. I only use the '86 Act as an example of how powerful some rules and laws can be. If a person is to be successful on the

'B' or 'I' side of the *Quadrant*, he or she needs to be aware of market forces and any changes in the law that affect those market forces.

Today in America, there are more than 100,000 pages of tax code. That's for the IRS alone. The federal laws come to more than 1.2 million pages of laws. It would take the average reader 23,000 years to read the entire U.S. Code. Every year more laws are created, deleted and changed. It would be more than a full-time job just to keep up with those changes.

Every time someone tells me, 'That's against the law,' I reply by asking them if they've read every line of code in America. If they say 'yes,' I leave slowly, backing up toward the door. Never turn your back on someone who thinks they know every law.

To be successful on the right side of the *Quadrant* requires seeing 5 percent with your eyes and 95 percent with your mind. Understanding the laws and market forces is vital for financial success. Great transfers of wealth often occur when laws and markets change. So it is important to pay attention if you want to have those changes work in your favor and not against you.

The Government Needs Your Money

I believe in paying taxes. I know the government provides many important and vital services essential for a well run civilization. Unfortunately, in my opinion, government is mismanaged, is too big, and has made too many promises it cannot keep. But it is not the fault of the politicians and lawmakers in office today, because most of the financial problems we face today were created more than 60 years ago by their predecessors. Today's lawmakers are trying to handle the problem and to find solutions. Unfortunately, if lawmakers want to stay in office, they cannot tell the masses the truth. If they did, they would be thrown out of office . . . because the masses still rely on the government to solve their financial and medical problems for them. Government cannot. Government is getting smaller, and the problems are getting bigger.

In the meantime, government will have to continue to come after more taxes . . . even if the politicians promise not to. That is why Congress passed the Tax Reform Act of 1986. It needed to plug a tax loophole in order to collect more in taxes. In the next few years, many of our Western governments must begin to collect even more in taxes to prevent a default on some of those promises made long ago. Promises made such as Medicare and Social Security, as well as federal pensions due to millions of federal workers. A mass public realization will probably not occur now, but the magnitude of the problem will be apparent by 2010. The world will realize that the U.S. will not be able to borrow its way out of these problems.

Forbes magazine ran this projection about the escalating U.S. debt:

'If you notice, it goes down until 2010, and then it zooms up. It zooms up just as the biggest group of people in the history of America begins to retire. In the year 2010, the first baby boomers turn 65. In the year 2010, instead of adding money to the stock market, baby boomers will begin withdrawing money from the stock market . . . if not earlier. By the year 2010, 75 million baby boomers will decide that their biggest 'asset,' their home, is too big since the kids are gone, and will begin selling their big houses so they can move to a more crime-free part of the country, small-town America.'

Suddenly, the current retirement vehicles, called the 401(k)s in America, or The Superannuation Funds in many Commonwealth countries, will begin to shrink. They will shrink because they are subject to market fluctuations . . . which means they go up with the market and they come down with the market. Mutual funds will begin to liquidate their stocks in order to pay for the sell orders from baby boomers needing to use the money for retirement. Baby boomers will suddenly be stuck with huge capital-gains taxes from the gains accrued by these mutual funds and taxable to them on withdrawal. The capital gains will come from selling these overvalued stocks at higher prices, which the funds pass on to its members. Instead of cash, many baby boomers will be stuck with a tax bill for capital gains they never received. Remember, the tax man always gets the money first.

Simultaneously, the health of millions of poorer baby boomers will begin to fail because poor people historically have worse health than affluent people. Medicare will be bankrupt and the cry for more government support will go up in cities all across America.

Add to this the eclipsing of America by China as the nation with the largest GNP and the advent of the European Monetary Union. I suspect that both wages and the prices of goods will have to come down . . . and/or productivity must skyrocket in order to meet the challenges of these two large economic blocks.

All this will happen by 2010, which is not too far away. The next great transfer of wealth will take place, not by conspiracy but by ignorance. We are in the final gasp of the entitlement mentality of big government and big business of the Industrial Age, and we are officially entering the Information Age. In 1989, the Berlin Wall came down. In my opinion, that event was as significant as the year 1492, when Columbus bumped into the Americas in his search for Asia. In some circles, 1492 was the official beginning of the Industrial Age. The end was marked in 1989. The rules have changed.

History Is A Guide

My rich dad encouraged me to learn the game well. After I learned it well, then I could do what I wanted with what I knew. I write and teach out of concern and a sense that more people need to know how to take care of themselves financially . . . and not become dependent upon the government or a company for life support.

I hope I am wrong about what I see coming down the road economically. Maybe governments can keep making promises to take care of people: keep on raising taxes, and keep on going into greater debt. Maybe the stock market will always go up and never come down again . . . and maybe real estate prices will always go up and your home will become your best investment. And maybe millions of people will find happiness earning a minimum wage and be able to provide a good life for their family. Maybe this can all happen. But I don't think so. Not if history is any guide.

Historically, if people lived to be 75 years of age, they lived through two recessions and one depression. As baby boomers we have gone through two recessions, but we have not yet seen that depression. Maybe there will never be a depression again. But history does not say that. The reason my rich dad had me read books on the great capitalists and the economists was so that I could gain a longer view and a better perspective on where we have come from and where we are going.

Just as there are waves on the ocean, there are great waves in markets. Instead of the wind and sun driving the waves of the ocean, the waves of the financial markets are driven by two human emotions: greed and fear. I do not think that depressions are things of the past because we are all human beings and we will always have those emotions of greed and fear. And when greed and fear collide, and a person loses badly, the next human emotion is depression. Depression is made up of the two human emotions, anger and sadness. Anger with one's self and sadness over the loss. Economic depressions are emotional depressions. People lose and they get depressed.

Even though the economy overall may appear to be in great shape, there are millions of people who are in various stages of depression. They may have a job, but deep down they know they aren't getting ahead financially. They are angry at themselves and sad over their loss of time. Little do most know that they have been trapped by the Industrial Age idea of 'find a safe, secure job, and don't worry about the future.'

A Great Change . . . And Opportunity

We are entering into the era of tremendous change and opportunity. For some people, it will be the best of times and for others it will be the worst of times.

President John Kennedy said: 'A great change is at hand.'

Kennedy was a man who came from the 'B-I' side of the *Quadrant*, and he tried desperately to elevate the lives of those stuck in time warps. Unfortunately, millions of people are still in those time warps, following ideas in their heads that were handed down from ages past. Ideas such as 'go to school so you can find a secure job.' Education is more important than ever before, but we need to teach people to think a little further than just looking for a secure job and expecting the company or the government to look after them once their working days are through. That is an Industrial Age idea . . . and we aren't there anymore.

Nobody said it was fair . . . for this is not a fair country. We are a free country. There are people who work harder, are smarter, are more driven for success, are more talented, or are more desirous of the good life than others. We are free to pursue those ambitions if we have the determination. Yet every time somebody does better, some people say it is unfair. The same people think that it would be fair if the rich shared with the poor. Well, nobody said it was fair. And the more we try to make things fair, the less free we become.

When someone says to me that there is racial discrimination or a 'glass ceiling,' I agree with them. I know such things exist. I personally detest any kind of discrimination and, being of Japanese ancestry, I have experienced discrimination firsthand. On the left side of the *Quadrant*, discrimination does exist, especially in companies. Your looks, your school, whether you're white or black or brown or yellow, or are male or female . . . all of those things count on the left side of the *Quadrant*. But they do not count on the right side of the *Quadrant*. The right side is concerned not with fairness or security, but with freedom and the love of the game. If you want to play the game on the right side, the players will welcome you. If you play and win, fine. They will welcome you even more and ask you for your secrets. If you play and lose, they will gladly take all your money, but don't complain or blame someone else for your failures. That is not the way the game is played on the right side of the *Quadrant*. It is not meant to be fair. Being fair is not the name of the game.

So Why Does Government Leave The 'B-I' Side Alone?

In reality, governments do not leave the 'B-I' side alone. It is more that the 'B-I' side has more ways of escaping and hiding wealth. In *Rich Dad Poor Dad*, I talked about the power of corporations. One big reason the rich keep more of their wealth is simply because they operate as corporate bodies and not human bodies. A human body needs a passport to go from country to country. A corporate body does not. A corporate body travels the world freely and can often work freely. A human body needs to register with the government, and in America they need a 'green card' to work. A corporate body does not.

While governments would like to take more money from corporate bodies they realize that if they pass abusive tax laws, the corporate bodies will take both their money and their jobs to some other country. In the Industrial Age, people talked about 'off-shore' as a country. The rich have always sought tax havens where their money would be treated kindly. Today, 'off-shore' is not a country; it is cyberspace. Money, being an idea and invisible, can now hide in the invisible, or at least out of sight from the human eye. Soon, if it is not already being done, people will do their banking on a geo-synchronous satellite orbiting in space . . . free from any laws, or they may choose to operate in a country whose laws are more favorable to rich people.

In *Rich Dad Poor Dad*, I wrote that corporations became popular at the start of the Industrial Age . . . just after Columbus discovered a new world filled with riches. Each time the rich sent a vessel out to sea they were at risk because if the ship did not come back the rich did not want to be indebted to the families of the sailors who died. So corporations were formed for legal protection and to limit the risk of loss to the amount of money ventured, and not beyond that. So the rich risked only their money, and the crews risked their lives. Not much has changed since then.

Wherever I travel in the world, the people I deal with primarily deal in this manner . . . as employees of their own corporations. In theory, they own nothing and really do not exist as private citizens. They exist as officers of their rich corporations, but as private citizens they own nothing. And wherever I go in the world, I meet people who tell me, 'You can't do that in this country. That is against the law.'

Little do most people realize that most countries' laws in the Western world are similar. They may use different words to describe the same things, but in principle, their laws are pretty much the same.

I recommend that, if possible, you at least consider being an employee of your own corporation. It is especially advisable for high income 'S's' and for 'B's,' even if they own franchises or earn their income from network marketing. Seek advice from competent financial advisers. They can help you choose and implement the best structure for your particular situation.

There Are Two Kinds Of Laws

On the surface, it seems as if there are laws for the rich and there are laws for everyone else. But in reality, the laws are the same.

222

The only difference is the rich use the laws to their advantage while the poor and middle class do not. That is the fundamental difference. The laws are the same . . . they are written for everyone . . . and I strongly suggest you hire smart advisers and obey the laws. It's too easy to make money legally rather than break the laws and wind up in jail. Besides, your legal advisers will serve as your early warning system for upcoming law changes . . . and when laws change, wealth changes hands.

Two Choices

One advantage of living in a free society is the freedom to make choices. In my opinion, there are two big choices . . . the choice of security and the choice of freedom. If you choose security, there is a huge price to pay for that security in the form of excessive taxes and punishing interest payments. If you choose freedom, then you need to learn the whole game and then play the game. It is your choice which quadrant you want to play the game from.

Part I of this book defined the specifics of the *CASHFLOW Quadrant*, while Part II has focused on developing the mind-set and attitude of someone who chooses the right side of the *Quadrant*. So now you should understand where you are currently in the *Quadrant*, as well as have an idea of where you want to be. You also should have a better understanding of the mental process and mind-set of operating from the right side of the *Quadrant*.

While I have shown you ways to cross from the left side to the right side of the *Quadrant*, I now would like to provide you with more specifics. In the final section of the book, Part III, I will identify 7 steps to finding your financial fast track that I consider to be essential in moving to the right side of the *Quadrant*.

AUTHOR'S NOTE

In 1943, the U.S. began taxing all working Americans via pay roll deduction. In other words, the government got paid before people in the 'E' quadrant got paid. Anyone who was purely an 'E' had little escape from the government. It also meant that instead of only the rich being taxed, which was the hope of the 16th Amendment, it now meant everyone on the left side of the *Quadrant* got taxed, rich or poor. As stated earlier, the lowest paid in America today pay more in taxes as a percentage of total income than the rich and the middle class.

In 1986, the Tax Reform Act went after the highly paid professionals in the 'S' quadrant. The act specifically listed doctors, lawyers, architects, dentists, engineers, and other such professions, and made it difficult, if not impossible, for them to shelter their income the way that the rich can do in the 'B' and 'I' quadrants.

These professionals were forced to operate their businesses through S corporations instead of through C corporations, or pay a tax penalty. The rich do not pay this penalty. Income for these highly compensated professionals is then passed through the S corporation and taxed at the highest individual tax rate possible. They don't have the opportunity to shelter their income through deductions allowed to a C corporation. And, at the same time, the law was changed to force all S corporations to have a calendar year end. This again forced all income to be taxed at the highest rate.

When I was discussing these changes recently with my personal CPA, she reminded me that the biggest shock to newly self-employed people generally comes at the end of their first business year when they realize that the biggest tax they are paying is a 'self-employment' tax. This tax is double for 'S's', or self-employed, over what they paid as 'E's', or employees. And it is calculated based on income before the individual can deduct any itemized deductions or personal exemptions. It is possible for a self-employed person to have no taxable income, yet still owe self-employment tax. Corporations, on the other hand, do not pay self-employment tax.

The 1986 Tax Reform Act also effectively pushed the 'E's' and 'S's' of America out of real estate as an investment and into paper assets such as stocks and mutual funds. Once the downsizing began, millions not only felt less secure about their jobs, they also felt less secure about their retirement, simply because they were basing their future financial well-being upon paper assets subject to the ups and downs of the market.

The 1986 Tax Reform Act also appears to have had the intention of shutting down the smaller community banks in America and shifting all banking to large national banks. I suspect that the reason this was done was so that America could compete with the large banks of Germany and Japan. If that was the intent, it was successful. Today in America, banking is less personal and purely by the numbers, the net result being that it is harder for certain classes of people to qualify for home loans. Instead of a small town banker knowing you by your character, today a central computer spits your name out if you don't meet it's impersonal qualification requirements.

After the 1986 Tax Reform Act, the rich continue to earn more, work less, pay less in taxes, and enjoy greater asset protection by using the formula my rich dad gave me 40 years ago, which was, 'Build a business and buy real estate.' Make a lot of money via C corporations, and shelter your income through real estate. While millions upon millions of Americans work; pay more and more in taxes; and then pour billions each month into mutual funds, the rich are quietly selling the shares of their C corporations, making them even richer, and then buying billions

225

in investment real estate. A share of a C corporation allows the buyer to share in the risk of owning the company. A share of stock does not allow the shareholder the advantages that owning a C corporation and investing in real estate offers.

Why did my rich dad recommend building businesses in C corporations and then buying real estate? Because the tax laws reward people who operate that way . . . but this is a subject that is beyond the scope of this book. Just remember the words of such immensely wealthy people such as Ray Kroc, founder of McDonald's.

'My business is not hamburgers. My business is real estate.'

My rich dad, who drummed into my head,

'Build businesses and buy real estate.'

In other words, seek my fortune on the right side of the *CASH-FLOW Quadrant* to take full advantage of the tax laws.

In 1990, President George Bush raised taxes after promising, 'Watch my lips. No new taxes.' In 1992, President Clinton signed into law the largest tax increase in recent history. Again, those increases affected the 'E's' and 'S's' but the 'B's' and 'I's' were for the most part, not affected.

As we progress further and further away from the Industrial Age and into the Information Age, we all need to continue to gather information from different quadrants. In the Information Age, quality information is our most important asset. As Erik Hoffer once said,

> 'In times of change . . .
> Learners inherit the earth,
> While the learned
> Find themselves beautifully equipped
> to deal with a world
> that no longer exists.'

Remember

Everyone's financial situation is different. That is why I always recommend:

1. Seek out the best professional and financial advice you can find. For example while a C corporation may work well in some instances, it does not work well in all instances. Even on the right side of the *Quadrant*, occasionally an S corporation is appropriate.

2. Remember that there are different advisors for the rich, the poor, and the middle class, just as there are different advisors for people who earn their money on the right side and on the left. Also consider seeking advice from people who are already where you want to go.

3. Never do business or investing for tax reasons. A tax break is an extra bonus for doing things the way the government wants. It should be a bonus, not the reason.

4. If you are a reader who is not a U.S. citizen, this advice remains the same. Our laws may be different, yet the principles of seeking competent advice remain the same. People on the right side operate very similarly throughout the world.

PART THREE

HOW TO BECOME A SUCCESSFUL 'B' AND 'I'

CHAPTER TEN
Take Baby Steps

Most of us have heard the saying, 'A journey of a thousand miles begins with a single step.' I would like to modify that statement a little. Instead I would say, 'A journey of a thousand miles begins with a baby step.'

I emphasize this because I have seen too many people attempt to take the 'Great Leap Forward' instead of taking baby steps. We have all seen people, who are completely out of shape, suddenly decide to lose 20 pounds and get into shape. They begin a crash diet, go to the gym for two hours, and then jog 10 miles. This lasts maybe a week. They lose a few pounds, and then the pain, boredom, and hunger begin to wear away at their will power and determination. By the third week, their old habits of overeating, lack of exercise, and television are back in control.

Instead of taking a 'Great Leap Forward,' I would strongly recommend taking a baby step forward. Long term financial success is not measured in how big your stride is. Long term financial success is measured in the number of steps, in which direction you're moving and in numbers of years. In reality, that is the formula for success or failure in any endeavor. When it comes to money, I have seen too many people, myself included, attempt to do too much with too little . . . and then crash and burn. It's hard to take a baby step forward when you first need a ladder to get yourself out of the financial hole you have dug for yourself.

How Do You Eat An Elephant?

This section of the book describes 7 steps to guide you on your path to the right side of the *Quadrant*. With the guidance of my rich dad, I began working and acting on these 7 steps from the age of 9. I will continue to follow them for as long as I live. I warn you before you read the 7 steps because, for some people, the task may seem overwhelming and it will be if you try to do it all in one week. So please begin with baby steps.

We have all heard the saying, 'Rome was not built in a day.' The saying I use whenever I find myself feeling overwhelmed by how much I have to learn is 'How do you eat an elephant?' The answer is 'One bite at a time.' And that is how I would recommend you proceed if you find yourself feeling even a little bit overwhelmed by how much you may have to learn, in order to make the journey from the 'E' and 'S' side to the 'B' and 'I' side. Please be kind to yourself and realize that the transition is more than just mental learning, the process also involves emotional learning. After you can take baby steps for six months to a year, you are ready for the next saying which is, 'You've got to walk before you can run.' In other words you go from baby steps, to walking, and then to running. This is the path I recommend. If you don't like this path, then you can do what millions of people do who want to get rich quickly the fast and easy way, which is to buy a lottery ticket. Who knows? It might be your lucky day.

Action Beats Inaction

To me, one of the primary reasons 'E's' and 'S's' have difficulty moving to the 'B' and 'I' side is because they are too afraid of making mistakes. They often say, 'I have a fear of failing.' Or they say, 'I need more information, or can you recommend another book?' Their fear or self doubt is primarily what keeps them trapped in their quadrant. Please take the time to read the 7 steps and complete the action steps at the end of each step. That for most people is enough of a baby step to get you moving in the direction towards the 'B' and 'I' side. Just doing those 7 action steps will open whole new worlds of possibility and change. Then just keep taking small baby steps.

Nike's slogan 'Just do it' says it best. Unfortunately our schools also say, 'Don't make mistakes.' Millions of highly educated people who want to take action are paralyzed by the emotional fear of making mistakes. One of the most important lessons I have learned as a teacher is that true learning requires mental, emotional, and physical learning. That is why action always beats inaction. If you take action and make a mistake, at least you've learned something be it mentally, emotionally, and/or physically. A person who continually searches for the 'right' answer is often afflicted with the disease known as 'analysis paralysis' which seems to affect many well-educated people. Ultimately, the way we learn is by making mistakes. We learned to walk and ride a bicycle by making mistakes. People who are afraid of taking action, out of fear of making mistakes, may be mentally smart but emotionally and physically handicapped.

There was a study done a number of years ago of rich and poor all around the world. The study wanted to find out how people born into poverty eventually become wealthy. The study found that these people, regardless of in which country they lived, possessed three qualities. These qualities were:

1. They maintained a long term vision and plan.
2. They believed in delayed gratification.
3. They used the power of compounding in their favor.

The study found that these people thought and planned for the long term and knew that they could ultimately achieve financial success by holding to a dream or a vision. They were willing to make short term sacrifices to gain long-term success, the basis of delayed gratification. Albert Einstein was amazed at how money

233

could multiply just by the power of compounding. He considered the compounding of money as one of the most amazing inventions of humans. This study took compounding to another level beyond money. The study reinforced the idea of baby steps . . . because each baby step in learning compounded over the years. People who had taken no steps at all did not have the leverage of magnified accumulation of knowledge and experience that comes from compounding.

The study also found what caused people to go from wealthy to poor. There are many rich families who lose most of their wealth after only three generations. Not surprisingly the study found that these people possessed the following three qualities:

1. They have short term vision.
2. They have a desire for instantaneous gratification.
3. They abuse the power of compounding.

Today I meet people who get frustrated with me because they want me to tell them how they can make more money today. They do not like the idea of thinking long term. Many are desperately seeking short term answers because they have money problems to be solved today . . . money problems such as consumer debt and lack of investments caused by their uncontrolled desire for instantaneous gratification. They have the idea of 'Eat, drink, and be merry while we're young.' This abuses the power of compounding, which leads to long-term debt, instead of long-term wealth.

They want the quick answer and want me to tell them 'What to do.' Instead of hearing 'Who they need "to be" in order "to do" what they need to do to acquire great wealth,' they want short-term answers to a long-term problem. In other words, too many people are fixated upon the 'Get rich quick' philosophy of life. To these people I wish them luck because luck is what they will need.

A Hot Tip

Most of us have heard that people who write down their goals are more successful than those who do not. There is a teacher named Raymond Aaron, from Ontario, Canada who has seminars and tapes on subjects such as sales, goal setting, doubling your income, and how to be a better networker. While these are subjects taught by many people, I recommend his work simply because he has some fascinating insights into these important subjects. Insights that can help you achieve more of what you want in the world of business and investing.

On the subject of goal setting, he recommends something that follows in line with the idea of taking baby steps instead of great leaps forward. He recommends having great big long-term dreams and wishes. Yet, when it comes to setting goals, instead of trying to be an overachiever, he recommends being an underachiever. In other words, take baby steps. For example, if I wanted to have a beautiful body, instead of trying to take a great leap forward, he recommends underachieving by doing less than you would want to. Instead of going to the gym for one hour, commit to going for only 20 minutes. In other words, set an underachieving goal and force yourself to stick with it. The result will be instead of being overwhelmed, you will feel underwhelmed. By feeling underwhelmed, I have found myself looking forward to going to the gym, or anything else I need to do or change in my life. The strange thing is that I find I achieve today by being an underachiever instead of trying to kill myself and be an overachiever. In summary, dream big daring dreams, and then underachieve a little bit each day. In other words, baby steps instead of great leaps over the cliff. Set attainable daily goals that, when achieved, provide positive reinforcement to help you stay on the path to the big goal.

An example of the way I underachieve is that I set a written goal to listen to two audio cassette tapes a week. I may listen to the same tape two or more times if it's good . . . but it still counts towards my 2 cassettes a week. My wife and I also have a written goal to attend at least two seminars a year on subjects about the 'B' and 'I' quadrants. We go on vacations with people who are experts on subjects found in the 'B' and 'I' quadrants. Again we learn a lot while playing, resting, and dining out. Those are ways of underachieving and yet still moving towards big and bold dreams. I thank Raymond Aaron and his tape on goal setting for assisting me in achieving more with a lot less stress.

Now read on, and remember to dream big, think long-term, underachieve on a daily basis, and take baby steps. That is the key to long-term success and the key to crossing from the left side of the *CASHFLOW Quadrant* to the right side.

If You Want To Be Rich, You've Got To Change Your Rules

I have often been quoted as saying 'The rules have changed.' When people hear these words, they nod their head in agreement and say, 'Yes. The rules have changed. Nothing is the same anymore.' But then they go on and do the same old thing.

Industrial Age Financial Statements

When I teach classes on the topic of 'Getting Your Financial Life In Order,' I start by asking the students to fill out a personal financial statement. It often becomes a life-changing experience. Financial statements are much like X-rays. Both financial statements and X-rays let you see what your unassisted eye cannot. After the class members have filled out their statements, it is easy to see who has 'financial cancer' and who is financially healthy. Generally, the ones with financial cancer are those with Industrial Age ideas.

Why do I say that? Because in the Industrial Age, people did not have to 'think about tomorrow.' The rules were, 'Work hard and your employer or the government will take care of your tomorrows.' Which is why so many of my friends and family often said, 'Get a job with the government. It has great benefits.' Or: 'Make sure the company you work for has an excellent retirement plan.' Or: 'Make sure the company you work for has a strong union.' Those are words of advice based on Industrial Age rules, which I refer to as the 'entitlement' mentality. Although the rules have changed, many people have not changed their personal rules . . . especially their financial rules. They're still spending like there is no need to plan for tomorrow. That is what I look for when I read a person's financial statement – whether or not they have a tomorrow.

Do You Have A Tomorrow?

Keeping things simple – this is what I look for on a personal financial statement.

Income Statement

Income
Expense
(Today)

Balance Sheet

Assets	Liabilities
(Tomorrow)	(Yesterday)

People with no assets, which throw off cash flow, have no tomorrows. When I find people who have no assets, they generally are working hard for a paycheck to pay bills. If you look at most people's 'Expense column,' the two biggest monthly expenses are taxes and debt service for long-term liabilities. Their expense statements look like this:

Income Statement

Income
Expense
Taxes (Approximately 50%)
Debt (Approximately 35%)
Living Expenses

Balance Sheet

Assets	Liabilities

In other words, the government and the bank get paid before they do. People who cannot get control of their cash flow generally have no financial future and will find themselves in serious trouble in the next few years.

Why? A person who is only in the 'E' quadrant has little protection from taxes and debt. Even an 'S' can do something about these two financial cancers.

If this does not make sense to you, I would suggest reading or re-reading *Rich Dad Poor Dad*, which should make this and the next few chapters easier to understand.

Three Cash Flow Patterns

As stated in *Rich Dad Poor Dad*, there are three basic cash flow patterns: one for the rich, one for the poor, and one for the middle class. This is the cash flow pattern of the poor:

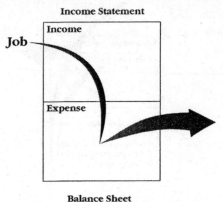

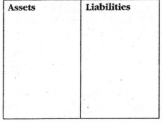

This is the cash flow pattern of the middle class.

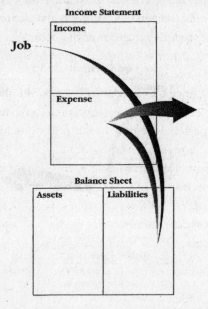

This cash flow pattern is considered 'normal' and 'intelligent' by our society. After all, the people who have this pattern probably have good high-paying jobs, nice homes, cars and credit cards. This is what my rich dad called the 'working-class dream.'

When I play my educational board game, *CASHFLOW*, with adults they usually struggle mentally. Why? Because they are being introduced to financial literacy, which means understanding the numbers and words of money. The game takes several hours to play, not because the game is long, but because the players are learning a completely new subject. It is almost like learning a foreign language. But the good news is that this new literacy can be learned quickly, and then the game picks up speed. It picks up speed because the players are smarter . . . and the more they play the game, the smarter and faster they become, all the while having fun.

Something else also happens. Because they are now becoming financially literate, many begin to realize that they are personally in financial trouble, even though the rest of society thinks they are 'financially normal.' You see, to have a middle class cash flow pattern was normal in the Industrial Age, but it could be disastrous in the Information Age.

Many people, once they successfully learn and understand the game, begin to seek new answers. It becomes a financial wake-up call about their personal financial health, just as a mild heart attack is an alert about a person's medical health.

At that moment of understanding, many people begin thinking like a rich person instead of a hard-working middle class person. After playing *CASHFLOW* several times, some people begin to change their thinking pattern to that of the rich, and they begin to seek a cash flow pattern that looks like this.

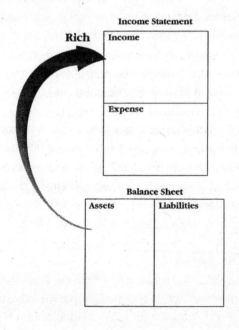

This is the mental thought pattern my rich dad wanted his son and me to have as young children, which is why he took away our paychecks and refused to give us raises. He never wanted us to become addicted to the idea of a high-paying job. He wanted us to develop the thought pattern of thinking only in assets and income in the form of capital gains, dividends, rental income, residual income from businesses, and royalties.

For people who want to be successful in the Information Age, the faster they begin to develop their financial intelligence and emotional intelligence to think in this pattern, the faster they will feel more financially secure and find financial freedom. In a world of less and less job security, this cash flow pattern makes much more sense to me. And to achieve this pattern a person needs to see the world from the 'B' and 'I' quadrants, not just the 'E' and 'S' quadrants.

I also call this an Information Age financial statement because the income is generated strictly from information, not hard work. In the Information Age, the idea of hard work does not mean the same thing as it did in the Agrarian Age and the Industrial Age. In the Information Age, the people who work physically the hardest will be paid the least. It is already true today and has been true through history.

However, today when people say, 'Don't work hard, work smart,' they do not mean work smart in the 'E' or 'S' quadrants. They actually mean work smart in the 'B' or 'I' quadrants. That is Information Age thinking which is why financial intelligence and emotional intelligence are vital today and will be vital in the future.

So What Is The Answer?

Obviously my answer is to re-educate yourself to think like a rich person, not a poor or middle class person. In other words, to think and look at the world from the 'B' or 'I' quadrant. However, the solution is not as simple as going back to school and taking a few courses. To be successful in the 'B' or 'I' quadrant requires financial intelligence, systems intelligence and emotional intelligence. These things cannot be learned in school.

The reason these intelligences are hard to learn is because most adults are 'wired' to the 'hard work and spend' mode of life. They feel financial anxiety, so they hurry off to work and work hard. They come home and hear about the stock market going up and down. The anxiety grows, so they go shopping for a new house or car, or they go and play golf to avoid the anxiety.

The problem is that the anxiety returns on Monday morning.

How Do You Start Thinking Like A Rich Person?

People often ask me how to get started thinking like a rich person. I always recommend starting small and seeking education, rather than running out and simply buying a mutual fund or a rental property. If people are serious about learning and retraining themselves to think like a rich person, I recommend my board game, *CASHFLOW*.

I created the game to help people improve their financial intelligence. It gives people the mental, physical and emotional training required to allow them to make the gradual change from thinking like a poor or middle class person to thinking like a rich person. It teaches people to think about what my rich dad said was important . . . which was not a large paycheck or big house.

Cash Flow, Not Money, Relieves Anxiety

Financial struggle and poverty are really financial anxiety problems. They are mental and emotional loops that keep people stuck in what I call the 'rat race.' Unless the mental and emotional hooks are broken, the pattern remains intact.

I worked with a banker a few months ago on breaking his pattern of financial struggle. I am not a therapist, but I have had experience in breaking my own financial habits instilled by my family.

This banker makes more than $120,000 a year, but is always in some sort of financial trouble. He has a beautiful family, three cars, a big house, a vacation home, and he looks the part of a prosperous banker. When I looked at his financial statement however, I found he had a financial cancer that would be terminal in a few years if he did not change his ways.

The first time he and his wife played *CASHFLOW*, he struggled and fidgeted almost uncontrollably. His mind was wandering, and he could not seem to grasp the game. After four hours of play, he was still stuck. Everyone else had completed the game, but he was still in the 'Rat Race'.

So I asked him, as we put the game away, what was going on. His only answer was that the game was too hard, too slow and too boring. I then reminded him of what I had told him before the game started: that all games are reflections of the people playing. In other words, a game is like a mirror that allows you to look at yourself.

That statement angered him, so I backed off, and asked if he was still committed to getting his financial life in order. He said he was still committed, so I invited him and his wife, who loved the game, to come play again with an investment group I was coaching.

A week later, he showed up reluctantly. This time, a few lights began to go on inside his head. For him, the accounting part was easy, so he was naturally neat and tidy with his numbers, which is important for the game to be valuable. But now he was beginning to understand the world of business and investing. He could finally 'see' with his mind his own life's patterns and what he was doing to cause his own financial struggle. He still did not finish the game after four hours, but he was beginning to learn. As he left this time, he invited himself back.

By the third meeting, he was a new man. He was now in control of the game, his accounting and his investments. His confidence soared, and this time he successfully exited the 'Rat Race' and was on the 'Fast Track.' This time as he left, he purchased a game and said, 'I'm going to teach my kids.'

By the fourth meeting, he told me his own personal expenses were down, he had changed his spending habits and cut up several credit cards, and he was now taking an active interest in learning to invest and build his asset column. His thinking was now on track to make him an Information Age thinker.

At the fifth meeting, he beta tested *CASHFLOW 202*, which is the advanced game for people who have mastered the original *CASHFLOW (101)*. He was now ready and eager to play the fast and risky game that true 'B's' and 'I's' play. The best news was that he had taken control of his financial future. This man was completely different from the one who had asked me to make *CASHFLOW* easier the first time he played it. I told him that if he wanted an easier game, he should play *Monopoly*, which is also an excellent teaching game. A few weeks later, instead of wanting things to be easier, he was actively seeking bigger challenges and he was optimistic about his financial future.

He had re-educated himself not only mentally but also – more importantly – emotionally, via the power of the repetitive learning process that comes from a game. In my opinion, games are a superior teaching tool because they require the player to become fully involved in the learning process, while having fun. Playing a game involves a person mentally, emotionally and physically.

THE 7 STEPS TO FINDING YOUR FINANCIAL FAST TRACK

CHAPTER ELEVEN

STEP 1:
It's Time To Mind
Your Own Business

Have you been working hard and making everyone else rich? Early in life, most people are programmed to mind other people's businesses and make other people rich. It begins innocently enough with words of advice such as these:

1. 'Go to school and get good grades, so you can find a safe, secure job with good pay and excellent benefits.'
2. 'Work hard so you can buy the home of your dreams. After all, your home is an asset and it is your most important investment.'
3. 'Having a large mortgage is good because the government gives you a tax deduction for your interest payments.'
4. 'Buy now, pay later,' or 'Low down, easy monthly payments.' Or, 'Come in and save money.'

People who blindly follow these words of advice often become:

1. Employees, making their bosses and owners rich.
2. Debtors, making banks and money lenders rich.

3. Taxpayers, making the government rich.
4. Consumers, making many other businesses rich.

Instead of finding their own financial fast track, they help everyone else find theirs. Instead of minding their own business, they work all their lives minding everyone else's.

By looking at the Income Statement and Balance Sheet, you can easily begin to see how we have been programmed from an early age to mind everyone else's business, and ignore our own business.

Income Statement

Income
1. You mind your boss's business.
Expense
2. You mind the government's business via taxes. With every other line item expense, you mind a lot of other people's businesses.

Balance Sheet

Assets	**Liabilities**
4. This is your business.	3. You mind your banker's business.

Take Action

In my classes, I often ask people to fill out their financial statements. For many people, their financial statements are not a pretty picture simply because they've been misled into minding everyone else's business instead of minding their own business.

1) YOUR FIRST STEP:

Fill out your own personal financial statement. I have included a sample income statement and balance sheet as shown in the game, *CASHFLOW*.

In order to get where you want to go you need to know where you are. This is your first step to take control of your life and spend more time minding your own business.

2) SET FINANCIAL GOALS:

Set a long-term financial goal for where you want to be in 5 years and a smaller, short-term financial goal for where you want to be in 12 months. (The smaller financial goal is a stepping stone along the way to your 5-year goal.) Set goals that are realistic and attainable.

A) Within the next twelve months:

1. I want to decrease my debt by $_____.
2. I want to increase my cash flow from my assets, or passive income, (passive income is income you earn without you working for it) to $_____ per month.

B) My 5-year financial goals are:

1) Increase my cash flow from my assets to $_____ per month.
2) Have these investment vehicles in my asset column (i.e. real estate, stocks, businesses, etc.) _____
_____
_____

C) Use your 5-year goals to develop your income statement and balance sheet for 5 years from today.

Now that you know where you are financially today and have set your goals, you need to get control of your cash flow so that you can achieve your goals.

Profession _____ **Player** _____

Goal: To get out of the Rat Race and onto the Fast Track by building up your Passive Income to be greater than your Total Expenses

Income Statement

Income

Salary:	
Interest:	
Dividends:	
Real Estate:	Cash Flow
Businesses:	Cash Flow

Auditor _____

Person on your right

Passive Income= _____
(Interest + Dividends +
Real Estate + Business Cash Flows)

Total Income: _____

Expenses

Taxes:	
Home Mortgage:	
School Loan Payment:	
Car Payment:	
Credit Card Payment:	
Retail Payment:	
Other Expenses:	
Child Expenses:	
Bank Loan Payment:	

Number of
Children: _____
(Begin game with 0 Children)
Per Child
Expense: _____

Total Expenses: _____

Monthly Cash Flow: _____
(Pay Check)

Balance Sheet

Assets

Savings:		
Stocks/Mutual's/CD's	No. of Shares:	Cost/Share:
Real Estate:	Down Pay:	Cost:
Business:	Down Pay:	Cost:

Liabilities

Home Mortgage:	
School Loans:	
Car Loans:	
Credit Cards:	
Retail Debt:	
RE Mortgage:	
Liability: (Business)	
Bank Loan:	

CHAPTER TWELVE

STEP 2:
Take Control Of
Your Cash Flow

Many people believe that simply making more money will solve their money problems but, in most cases, it only causes bigger money problems.

The primary reason most people have money problems is they were never schooled in the science of cash flow management. They were taught how to read, write, drive cars and swim, but they were not taught how to manage their cash flow. Without this training they wind up having money problems, then work harder believing that more money will solve the problem.

As my rich dad often said, 'More money will not solve the problem, if cash flow management is the problem.'

The Most Important Skill

After deciding to mind your own business, the next step as the CEO of the business of your life, is to take control of your cash flow. If you do not, making more money will not make you richer . . . in fact, more money makes most people poorer because they often go out and get deeper into debt every time they get a pay raise.

Who is Smarter – You Or Your Banker?

The majority of people do not prepare personal financial statements. At most, they try to balance their checkbooks each month. So congratulate yourself, you are now ahead of most of your colleagues simply by completing your financial statement and setting goals for yourself.

As CEO of your own life, you can learn to be smarter than most people, even your banker.

Most people will say that 'two sets of books' is illegal. And that is true in some instances. Yet, in reality, if you truly understand the world of finances, there must always be two sets of books. Once you realize this, you will be as smart, and maybe smarter, than your banker. The following is an example of a legal 'two sets of books' – yours and your banker's.

As CEO of your life, always remember these simple words and diagrams from my rich dad, who often said, 'For every liability you have, you are somebody else's asset.'

And he would draw this simple diagram.

Your Balance Sheet

Assets	Liabilities
	Mortgage

Your Bank's Balance Sheet

Bank's Balance Sheet

Assets	Liabilities
Your Mortgage	

As CEO of your life, you must always remember that for each of your liabilities, or debts, you are someone else's asset. That is the real 'two sets of books accounting.' For every liability, such as a mortgage, car loan, school loan and credit card, you're an employee of the people lending the money. You're working hard to make someone else rich.

Good Debt And Bad Debt

Rich dad often cautioned me about 'good debt and bad debt.' He would often say, 'Every time you owe someone money, you become an employee of their money. If you take out a 30 year loan, you've become a 30 year employee, and they do not give you a gold watch when the debt is retired.'

Rich dad did borrow money, but he did his best to not become the person who paid for his loans. He would explain to his son and me that good debt was debt that someone else paid for you, and bad debt was debt that you paid for with your own sweat and blood. That is why he loved rental properties. He would encourage me to buy rental property because 'the bank gives you the loan, but your tenant pays for it.'

Income And Expense

Not only do the two sets of books apply to assets and liabilities, but they also apply to income and expenses. The more complete verbal lesson from my rich dad was this: 'For most every asset, there must be a liability, but they do not appear on the same set of financial statements. For every expense, there must also be income, and again they do not appear on the same set of financial statements.'

This simple drawing will make that lesson clearer:

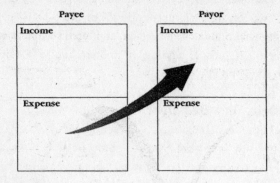

Most people cannot get ahead financially because every month, they have bills to pay. They have phone bills, tax bills, electric bills, gas bills, credit card bills, food bills, and so forth. Every month, most people pay everyone else first and pay themselves last, if they have anything left over. Hence, most people violate the golden rule of personal finance, which is, 'Pay yourself first.'

That is why rich dad stressed the importance of cash flow management and basic financial literacy. Rich dad would often say, 'People who cannot control their cash flow work for those who can.'

The Financial Fast Track And The Rat Race

The concept of 'two sets of books' can be used to show you the 'Financial Fast Track' and the 'Rat Race'. There are many different types of financial fast tracks. The diagram below is one of the most common. It is the track between a creditor and a debtor.

It is overly simplified, yet if you take time to study it, your mind will begin to see what most people's eyes cannot. Study it and you will see the relationship between the rich and the poor, the haves and have nots, the borrowers and the lenders, and those who create jobs and those who look for jobs.

This Is The Financial Fast Track And You're Already On It

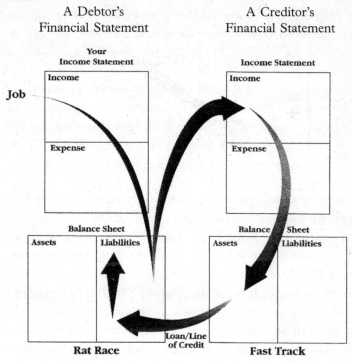

A Debtor's
Financial Statement

A Creditor's
Financial Statement

At this point, the creditor will say, 'Because of your good credit, we'd like to offer you a bill consolidation loan.' Or: 'Would you like to open a line of credit just in case you need some extra money in the future?'

Do You Know The Difference?

The path of money flowing between the two sets of books is what my rich dad called the 'Financial Fast Track.' It is also the 'Financial Rat Race.' For one to exist, so must the other. Hence, there must be at minimum two financial statements. The question is, which one is yours? And which one do you want to have?

This is why my rich dad constantly told me, 'Making more money will not solve your problems, if cash flow management is the problem,' and 'the people who understand the power of financial numbers have power over those who do not.'

This is why Step No. 2 to finding your own financial fast track is, 'Take control of your cash flow.'

You need to sit down and map out a plan to get control of your spending habits. Minimize your debt and liabilities. Live within your means before you try to increase your means. If you need assistance seek the help of a qualified financial planner. He or she can help you lay out a plan where you can improve your cash flow and start to pay yourself first.

Take Action

1) Review your financial statements from the previous chapter.

2) Determine which quadrant of the *CASHFLOW Quadrant* you receive your income from today._____

3) Determine which quadrant you want to receive the bulk of your income from in five years._____

4) Begin Your Cashflow Management Plan:

A) Pay yourself first. Put aside a set percentage from each paycheck or each payment you receive from other sources. Deposit that money into an investment savings account. Once your money goes into the account, NEVER take it out, until you are ready to invest it.

Congratulations! You have just started managing your cash flow.

B) Focus on reducing your personal debt.

The following are some simple and ready-to-apply tips for reducing and eliminating your personal debt.

Tip #1: If you have credit cards with outstanding balances . . .
     1. Cut up all your credit cards, except for 1 or 2.
     2. Any new charges you add to the 1 or 2 cards you now have must be paid off every month. Do not incur any further long-term debt.

Tip #2: Come up with $150–$200 extra per month. Now that you are becoming more and more financially literate this should be relatively easy to do. If you cannot generate an additional $150–$200 per month then your chances for financial freedom may only be a pipe dream.

Tip #3: Apply the additional $150–$200 to your monthly payment of ONLY ONE of your credit cards. You will now pay the minimum PLUS the $150–$200 on that one credit card.

     Pay only the minimum amount due on all other credit cards. Often people try to pay a little extra each month on all their cards, but those cards surprisingly never get paid off.

Tip #4: Once the first card is paid off, then apply the total amount you were paying each month on that card to your next credit card. You are now paying the minimum amount due on the second card PLUS the total monthly payment you were paying on your first credit card.

     Continue this process with all your credit cards and other consumer credit such as store charges, etc. With each debt you pay off, apply the full amount you were paying on that debt to the minimum payment of your next debt. As you pay off each debt, the monthly amount you are paying on the next debt will escalate.

Tip #5: Once all your credit cards and other consumer debt is paid off, now continue the procedure with your car and house payments.

If you follow this procedure you will be amazed at the shortened amount of time it takes for you to be completely debt-free. Most people can be debt-free within 5 to 7 years.

Tip #6: Now that you are completely debt-free, take the monthly amount you were paying on your last debt, and put that money towards investments. Build your asset column.

That's how simple it is.

CHAPTER THIRTEEN

STEP 3: Know The Difference Between Risk And Risky

I often hear people saying, 'Investing is risky.'

I disagree. Instead I say, 'Being uneducated is risky.'

What Is Proper Cash Flow Management?

Proper cash flow management begins with knowing the difference between an asset and a liability . . . and not the definition your banker gives you.

The following diagram is a picture of an individual who is 45 years old and who has properly managed his or her cash flow.

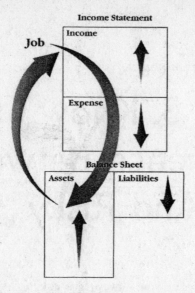

I use the age 45 because it is halfway between the age 25, when most people begin to work and 65, the age when most people plan on retiring. By age 45, if they have properly managed their cash flow, their asset column should be longer than their liability column.

This is a financial picture of people who take risks, but are not risky.

They are also in the upper 10 percent of the population. But if they do what the other 90 percent of the population does, which is mismanage their cash flow and not know the difference between an asset and a liability, their financial picture looks like this at age 45:

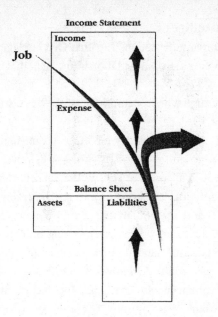

These are the people who most often say, 'Investing is risky.' For them, that statement is true – but not because investing is risky. It is their lack of formal financial training and knowledge that is risky.

Financial Literacy

In *Rich Dad Poor Dad*, I told the story of how my rich dad demanded that I become financially literate.

Financial literacy is simply looking at the numbers with your eyes, but it is also your trained mind that tells you which way the cash is flowing. Rich dad often said, 'The direction of cash flow is everything.'

So a house could be an asset or a liability depending on the direction of the cash flow. If the cash flows into your pocket, it is an asset, and if it flows out of your pocket, it is a liability.

Financial Intelligence

Rich dad had many definitions for 'financial intelligence,' such as 'the ability to convert cash or labor into assets that provide cash flow.'

But one of his favorite definitions was, 'Who is smarter? You or your money?'

To my rich dad, to spend your life working hard for money only to have it go out as fast as it comes in is not a sign of high intelligence. You may want to review the cash flow patterns of a poor person, a middle-class person and a rich person as presented in Chapter 10 and remember that a rich person focuses his or her efforts on acquiring assets, not working harder.

Due to the lack of financial intelligence, many educated people will put themselves into positions of high financial risk. My rich dad called it 'financial red line,' meaning income and expenses are nearly the same every month. These are the people who cling desperately to job security, are unable to change when the economy changes, and often destroy their health with stress and worry. And these are often the same people who say: 'Business and investing is risky.'

In my opinion, business and investing is not risky. Being under-educated is. Similarly, being misinformed is risky and relying on a 'safe secure job' is the highest risk anyone can take. Buying an asset is not risky. Buying liabilities you have been told are assets is risky. Minding your own business is not risky. Minding everyone else's business and paying them first is risky.

So Step 3 is to know the difference between risk and risky.

Take Action

1) Define risk in your own words.
a) Is relying on a paycheck risky to you?
b) Is having debt to pay each month risky to you?

c) Is owning an asset that generates cash flow into your pocket each month risky to you?

d) Is spending time to learn about financial education risky to you?

e) Is spending time learning about different types of investments risky to you?

2) Commit 5 hours of your time each week to do one or more of the following:

a) Read the business page of your newspaper and the *Wall Street Journal*.

b) Listen to the financial news on television or radio.

c) Listen to educational cassettes on investing and financial education.

d) Read financial magazines and newsletters.

e) Play *CASHFLOW*.

CHAPTER FOURTEEN

STEP 4: Decide What Kind Of Investor You Want To Be

Have you ever wondered why some investors make more money with a lot less risk than others?

Most people struggle financially because they avoid financial problems. One of the biggest secrets my rich dad taught me was this: 'If you want to acquire great wealth quickly, take on great financial problems.'

In Section I of this book, I went into the 7 levels of investors. I would like to add one more distinction that defines the three different types of investors:

Type A: Investors who seek problems.

Type B: Investors who seek answers.

Type C: Sgt. Schultz investors: 'I know nothing.'

Type C Investors

The name Sgt. Schultz comes from the lovable character in the TV series *Hogan's Heroes*. In the program, Sgt. Schultz is a guard in a German POW camp who knows the POWs are trying to escape or sabotage the German war effort.

When he knows something is wrong, all Schultz says is, 'I know nothing.' Most people, when it comes to investing, take the same attitude.

Can Sgt. Schultz investors still achieve great wealth? The answer is yes. They can get a job with the federal government, marry someone rich, or win the lottery.

Type B Investors

Type B investors often ask such questions as:

'What do you recommend I invest in?'

'Do you think I should buy real estate?'

'What mutual funds are good for me?'

'I talked to my broker and he recommended I diversify.'

'My parents gave me a few shares of stock. Should I sell them?'

Type B investors should immediately interview several financial planners, choose one and start taking their advice. Financial planners, if they're good, provide excellent technical knowledge and can often help you establish a financial game plan for your life.

The reason I do not offer specific financial advice in my books is because everyone's financial position is different. A financial planner can best evaluate where you are today, and then give you an idea on how to become a Level 4 investor.

An interesting side note – I often find that many high income 'E's' and 'S's' fall into the Type B investor category because they have little time to spend looking for investment opportunities. Because they are so busy, they often have little time to learn about the right side of the *Quadrant*. Hence, they seek answers rather than knowledge. So this group often buys what the Type A investor calls 'retail investments,' which are investments that have been packaged for sale to the masses.

Type A Investors

Type A investors look for problems. In particular they look for problems caused by those who get into financial trouble. Investors who are good at solving problems expect to make returns of 25 percent to infinity on their money. They are typically Level 5 and Level 6 investors who have strong financial foundations. They possess the skills necessary to succeed as business owners and investors, and they use those skills to solve problems caused by people who lack such skills.

For example, when I first started investing, all I looked for were small condominiums and houses that were in foreclosure. I started with $18,000 of problems that had been created by investors who did not manage their cash flow well and ran out of money.

After a few years, I was still looking for problems, but this time, the numbers were bigger. Three years ago, I was working on acquiring a $30 million mining company in Peru. While the problem and numbers were bigger, the process was the same.

How To Get On The Fast Track Faster

The lesson is to start small and learn to solve problems, and you will eventually gain immense wealth as you become better at solving problems.

For those who wish to acquire assets faster, I again emphasize the need to first learn the skills of the 'B' and 'I' side of the *Quadrant*. I recommend learning how to build a business first, because a business provides vital educational experience, improves personal skills, provides cash flow to soften the ups and downs of the marketplace, and provides free time. It is the cash flow from my business that bought me the free time to begin looking for financial problems to solve.

Can You Be All Three Types Of Investors?

In reality, I operate as all three types of investors. I am a Sgt.

269

Schultz, or a Type C investor, when it comes to mutual funds or picking stocks. When I am asked, 'What mutual funds do you recommend?' or 'What stocks are you buying?' I turn into Sgt. Schultz and respond 'I know nothing.'

I do have a few mutual funds, but I really do not spend much time studying them. I can achieve better results with my apartment houses than with mutual funds. As a type B investor, I seek professional answers to my financial problems. I seek answers from financial planners, stockbrokers, bankers and real estate brokers. If they are good, these professionals provide a wealth of information I do not personally have the time to acquire. They are also closer to the market and are, I trust, more up to date with changes in the laws and the markets.

The advice from my financial planner is priceless simply because she knows trusts, wills and insurance far better than I ever will. Everyone should have a plan, and that is why there is a financial planning profession. There is much more to investing than simply buying and selling.

I also give my money to other investors to invest for me. In other words, I know other level 5 and level 6 investors who seek partners in their investments. These are individuals I personally know and trust. If they choose to invest in an area I know nothing about, such as low-income housing or large office buildings, I may choose to give my money to them because I know they are good at what they do and I trust their knowledge.

Why You Should Get Started Quickly

One of the main reasons I recommend people find their own financial fast track quickly and take getting rich seriously is because in America, and most of the world, there are two sets of rules, one for the rich and one for everyone else. Many laws are written against people stuck in the financial rat race. In the world of business and investing, which is the world I am most familiar with, I find it shocking how little the middle class knows when it comes to where its tax dollars are going. Although tax dollars are going to many worthwhile causes, many of the larger tax breaks, incentives and payments are going to the rich, while the middle class is paying for them.

For example, low-income housing in America is a huge problem and a political hot potato. To help solve this problem, city, state and federal governments offer substantial tax credits, tax breaks and subsidized rents to people who finance and build low-income housing. Just by knowing the laws, financiers and builders become wealthier by having taxpayers subsidize their investments in low-income housing.

Why It's Unfair

Thus, not only do most people on the left side of the *CASH-FLOW Quadrant* pay more in personal income tax, but they are often not able to participate in tax-advantaged investments. This may be one source for the saying 'the rich get richer.'

I know it's unfair, and I understand both sides of the story. I have met people who protest and write letters to the editor of their newspaper. Some people try to change the system by running for political office. I say it's much easier to simply mind your own business, take control of your cash flow, find your own financial fast track and get rich. I contend that it is easier to change yourself than to change the political system.

Problems Lead To Opportunities

Years ago, my rich dad encouraged me to develop my skills as a business owner and investor. He also said, 'Then practice solving problems.'

For years, that is all I have done. I solve business and investment problems. Some people prefer to call them challenges, yet I like to call them problems, because that is what they are, for the most part.

I think people like the word 'challenges' more than 'problems' because they think one word sounds more positive than the other. Yet, to me, the word 'problem' has a positive meaning, because I know that inside of every problem lies an 'opportunity,' and opportunities are what real investors are after. And with every financial or business problem I address, regardless of whether I solve the problem, I wind up learning something. I may learn something new about finance, marketing, people or legal affairs. I often meet new people who become invaluable assets on other projects. Many become lifelong friends which is a priceless bonus.

Find Your Fast Track

So for those of you who want to find your financial fast track, start by:

1. Minding your own business.
2. Taking control of your cash flow.
3. Knowing the difference between risk and risky.
4. Knowing the difference between a Type A, B and C investor, and choosing to be all three.

To get on the financial fast track, become an expert at solving a certain type of problem. Do not 'diversify,' as people who are only Type B investors are advised to do. Become an expert at solving that one type of problem, and people will come to you with money to invest. Then, if you are good and trustworthy, you will reach your financial fast track more quickly. Here are a few examples:

Bill Gates is an expert at solving software marketing problems. He is so good at it the federal government is after him. Donald Trump is an expert at solving problems in real estate. Warren Buffet is an expert at solving problems in business and the stock market, which in turn allows him to buy valuable stocks and manage a successful portfolio. George Soros is an expert at

272

solving problems resulting from market volatility. That is what makes him an excellent hedge-fund manager. Rupert Murdock is an expert at solving the business problems of global television networks.

My wife and I are pretty good at solving problems in apartment housing that will eventually pay off with passive income. We know little outside the realm of the small to medium-size apartment house market we primarily invest in, and we do not diversify. If I choose to invest in areas outside those arenas I become a Type B investor, which means I give my money to people who have an excellent track record in their fields of expertise.

I have one focused objective, and that is to 'mind my own business.' Although my wife and I do work for charities and help other people in their efforts, we never lose sight of the importance of minding our own business and continually adding to our asset column.

So to become rich quicker, become a student of the skills needed by a business owner and investor, and seek to solve bigger problems . . . because inside of big problems lie huge financial opportunities. That is why I recommend becoming a 'B' first, before becoming an 'I.' If you are a master of solving business problems, you will have excess cash flow and your knowledge of business will make you a much smarter investor. I've said it many times before, yet it is worth saying again: Many people come to the 'I' quadrant in hopes that investing will solve their financial problems. In most cases, it doesn't. Investing only makes their financial problems worse if they are not already sound business owners.

There is no scarcity of financial problems. In fact, there is one right around the corner from you, waiting to be solved.

Take Action
GET EDUCATED IN INVESTING:
Once again, I recommend you become proficient as a level 4

investor before trying to become a level 5 or 6 investor. Start small and continue your education.

Each week do at least two of the following:

1. Attend financial seminars and classes. (I attribute much of my success to a real estate course I took as a young man that cost me $385. It has earned me millions over the years because I took action.)

2. Look for real estate 'for sale' signs in your area. Call on three or four per week and ask the sales person to tell you about the property. Ask questions like: Is it an investment property?

   If it is:

   Is it rented? What is the current rent? What is the vacancy rate? What are the average rents in that area? What are the maintenance costs? Is there deferred maintenance? Will the owner finance? What type of financing terms are available?

   Practice calculating the monthly cash flow statement for each property and then go over it with the agent for the property to see what you forgot. Each property is a unique business system and should be viewed as an individual business system.

3. Meet with several stockbrokers and listen to the companies they recommend for stock buys. Then research these companies at the library or over the internet. Call the companies and ask for their annual reports.

4. Subscribe to investment newsletters and study them.

5. Continue to read, listen to tapes & videos, watch financial TV programs, and play *CASHFLOW*.

GET EDUCATED IN BUSINESS:

1. Meet with several business brokers to see what existing businesses are for sale in your area. It is amazing the terminology you can learn by just asking questions and listening.

2. Attend a network marketing seminar to learn about its business system. (I recommend researching at least three different network marketing companies.)

3. Attend business opportunity conventions or trade expos in your area to see what franchises or business systems are available.

4. Subscribe to business newspapers and magazines.

CHAPTER FIFTEEN

STEP 5:
Seek Mentors

Who guides you to places you're never been to before?

A mentor is someone who tells you what is important and what is not important.

Mentors Tell Us What Is Important

The following is the score sheet from my educational board game, *CASHFLOW*. It was created to be a mentor, because it trains people to think like my rich dad thought and point out what he thought was financially important.

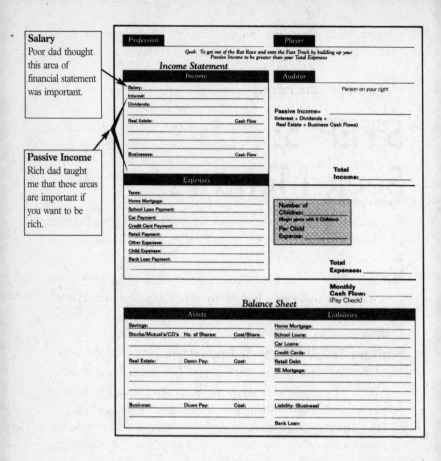

Salary
Poor dad thought this area of financial statement was important.

Passive Income
Rich dad taught me that these areas are important if you want to be rich.

My highly educated but poor dad thought that a job with a high salary was important, and that buying the house of your dreams was important. He also believed in paying bills first and living below your means.

My rich dad taught me to focus on passive income and spend my time acquiring the assets that provided passive or long-term residual income. He did not believe in living below your means. To his son and me, he often said, 'Instead of living below your means, focus on increasing your means.'

To do that, he recommended we focus on building the asset

column and increasing passive income from capital gains, dividends, residual income from businesses, rental income from real estate, and royalties.

Both dads served as strong mentors for me as I grew up. The fact that I chose to follow the financial advice of my rich dad did not lessen the impact that my educated but poor dad had on me as well. I would not be who I am today without the strong influence of both these men.

Reverse Role Models

Just as there are mentors who are excellent role models, there are people who are also reverse role models. In most instances, we all have both.

For example, I have a friend who has personally made more than $800 million in his lifetime. Today as I write, he is personally bankrupt. I have had other friends ask me why I continue to spend time with him. The answer to that question is because he is both an excellent role model and an excellent reverse role model. I can learn from both role models.

Spiritual Role Models

Both of my dads were spiritual men, yet when it came to money and spirituality, they had different points of view. For instance, they interpreted the saying 'the love of money is the root of all evil' differently.

My highly educated but poor dad felt any desire to have more money or to improve your financial position was wrong.

On the other hand, my rich dad interpreted this quote quite differently. He felt that temptation, greed and financial ignorance were wrong.

In other words, rich dad did not think money by itself was evil. He did believe that working all your life as a slave to money was evil and to be in financial slavery to personal debt was evil.

My rich dad often had a way of converting religious teachings into financial lessons, and I would like to share one of those lessons with you now.

The Power Of Temptation

Rich dad believed individuals who worked hard, were chronically in debt and lived beyond their means were poor role models for their children. Not only were they poor role models in his eyes, but he also felt that people in debt had given into temptation and greed.

He would often draw a diagram like the following and say:

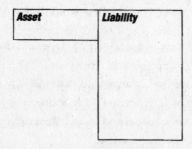

'And lead us not into temptation,' as he pointed to the liability column.

Rich dad believed that many financial problems came from the desire to possess items that had little value. When credit cards arrived, he foresaw that millions of people would go into debt and that the debt would eventually control their lives. We see people going into tremendous personal debt for homes, furnishings, clothes, vacations and cars, because they lacked control over that human emotion called 'temptation.' Today people work harder and harder, buying things they think are assets, but their spending habits will never allow them to acquire real assets.

He then would point to the asset column that follows and say,

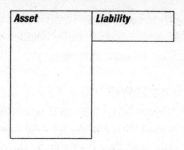

Asset	Liability

'But deliver us from evil.'

Which was rich dad's way of saying that delaying gratification (a sign of emotional intelligence), minding your own business, and building your asset column first would help you avoid the degradation of the human spirit caused by temptation, lack of financial education, and the influence of financially poor role models.

For those of you seeking your own personal fast track, I can only caution you to be careful about the people you are around every day. Ask yourself: Are they good role models? If not, I suggest consciously seeking to spend more time with people who are heading in the same direction you are.

If you cannot find them during working hours, you can find them in investment clubs, network marketing groups, and other business associations.

Find Someone Who's Been There

Choose your mentors wisely. Be careful from whom you take advice. If you want to go somewhere, it is best to find someone who has already been there.

For example, if you decide you are going to climb Mount Everest next year, obviously you'd seek advice from someone who had climbed the mountain before. However, when it comes to climbing financial mountains, most people ask advice from people who are also personally stuck in financial swamps.

The hard part of finding mentors who are 'B's' and 'I's' is that most people giving advice about those quadrants, and about money, are people who actually come from the 'E' and 'S' side of the *Quadrant*.

Rich dad encouraged me to always have a coach or mentor. He constantly said, 'Professionals have coaches. Amateurs do not.'

For example, I play golf and I take lessons, but I do not have a full-time coach. This is probably why I pay money to play golf instead of getting paid to play. Yet, when it comes to the game of business and investing, I do have coaches, several of them. Why do I have coaches? I have coaches because I get paid to play those games.

So choose your mentors wisely. It is one of the most important things you can do.

Take Action

1) Seek Mentors – Seek out individuals in both the investment and business arenas who might act as mentors to you.

   a) Seek out role models. Learn from them.

   b) Seek out reverse role models. Learn from them.

2) WHO YOU SPEND YOUR TIME WITH IS YOUR FUTURE

   a) Write down the six people you spend the most time with. All of your children count as one person. Remember that the qualifier is who you spend the most time with, not the type of your relationship. (DO NOT READ ANY FURTHER UNTIL YOU HAVE WRITTEN DOWN YOUR 6 NAMES.)

   I was at a seminar about fifteen years ago when the instructor asked us to do the same. I wrote down my 6 names.

282

He then asked us to look at the names we had written and announced, 'You are looking at your future. The six people you spend the most time with are your future.'

The six people you spend the most time with may not necessarily always be personal friends. For some of you it may be your co-workers, spouse and children, or members of your church or charity. My list was made up of co-workers, business associates, and rugby players. The list was pretty revealing once I began to look below the surface. I gained insights about myself that I liked and even more that I did not like.

The instructor had us go around the room and meet with other people to discuss our lists. After a while the relevance of the exercise began to sink in even deeper. The more I discussed my list with other people, and the more I listened to them, I realized that I needed to make some changes. This exercise had little to do with the people I was spending my time with. It had everything to do with where I was going and what I was doing with my life.

Fifteen years later, the people I spend the most time with are all different except one. The five others on my earlier list are still dear friends, but we rarely see each other. They are great people and they are happy with their lives. My change had only to do with me. I wanted to change my future. To successfully change my future, I had to change my thoughts, and as a result, the people I spent time with.

b) Now that you have your list of 6 people, the next step is: After each person's name list the quadrant they operate from.

Are they an 'E, S, B, or I'? A reminder: the quadrant reflects the way in which a person generates the majority of their income. If they are unemployed or retired, list the quadrant they earned their income in. Leave a blank for young children and students.

Note: A person can have more than one designation. For example, my wife, Kim, would have a 'B' and an 'I' next to her name since she generates 50% of her income from each.

So my list would have Kim at the top since she and I spend almost all of our time together.

NAME	Quadrant
1. Kim Kiyosaki	B-I
2.	
3.	
4.	
5.	
6.	

c) The next step is to list each person's level as an investor. Please refer to chapter 5 and the 7 Levels of Investors. Kim is a level 6 investor.

If you do not know a person's investor level, just do your best and take an educated guess.

So a name would be complete with the quadrant and investor level listed.

NAME	QUADRANT	INVESTOR LEVEL
1. Kim Kiyosaki	B-I	6
2.		
3.		
4.		
5.		
6.		

SOME PEOPLE GET ANGRY

I've had mixed reviews from people in doing this exercise. Some people get very angry. I have heard, 'How dare you ask me to classify the people around me?' So if this exercise has caused any emotional upset, please accept my apologies. This exercise is not intended to upset anyone. It is simply an exercise that is designed to shine some light on an individual's life. It does for some, but not for everyone.

When I did this exercise over 15 years ago, I realized that I was playing it safe and hiding. I was not happy with where I was and I used the people I worked with as the excuse as to why I was not making progress in my life. There were two people in particular that I argued with constantly, blaming them for holding our company back. My daily routine at work was to find their faults, point the faults out to them and then blame them for the problems we were having as an organization.

After completing this exercise, I realized that the two people I was always bumping heads with were very happy with where they were. I was the one who wanted to change. So instead of changing myself, I was pressuring them to change. After doing this exercise, I realized that I was projecting my personal expectations onto others. I wanted them to do what I did not want to do. I also thought that they should want and have the same things I did. It was not a healthy relationship. Once I realized what was happening, I was able to take the steps to change myself.

d) Take a look at the *CASHFLOW Quadrant* and place the initials of the people you spend time with in the appropriate quadrant.

Then put your initials in the quadrant you are in at present. Next put your initials in the quadrant you want to operate from in the future. If they are all primarily in the same quadrant, the chances are, you are a happy person. You are surrounded by like minded people. If they are not, you may want to consider some changes in your life.

CHAPTER SIXTEEN

STEP 6: Make Disappointment Your Strength

Who do you become when things do not go the way you want?

When I left the Marine Corps my rich dad recommended I get a job that taught me to sell. He knew I was shy. Learning to sell was the last thing in the world I wanted to do.

For two years I was the worst salesman in my company. I could not sell a life preserver to a drowning man. My shyness was painful not only to me but also to the customers I was trying to sell to. For those two years I was on and off probation which meant I was always on the verge of being fired.

Often I would blame the economy or the product I was selling, or even the customers, as the reasons for my lack of success. Rich dad had another way of looking at it. He would say, 'When people are lame, they love to blame.'

This meant that the emotional pain from the disappointment was so strong that the individual with the pain wants to push the pain onto someone else through blame. In order to learn to sell, I had to come face to face with the pain of disappointment. In the process of learning to sell, I found a priceless lesson: how to turn disappointment into an asset rather than a liability.

Whenever I meet people who are afraid to 'try' something new, in most cases the reason lies in their fear of being disappointed. They are afraid they might make a mistake, or get rejected. If you are prepared to embark on your journey to find your own financial fast track, I would like to offer you the same words of advice and encouragement my rich dad offered me when I was learning something new:

'Be prepared to be disappointed.'

He meant this in a positive sense, not a negative sense. His reasoning was that if you're prepared for disappointment, you have a chance of turning that disappointment into an asset. Most people turn disappointment into a liability – a long-term one. And you know it's long-term when you hear a person say, 'I'll never do that again.' Or: 'I should have known I would fail.'

Just as inside every problem lies an opportunity . . . inside every disappointment lies a priceless gem of wisdom.

Whenever I hear someone say, 'I'll never do that again,' I know I am listening to someone who has stopped learning. They have let disappointment stop them. Disappointment has turned into a wall erected around them, instead of a foundation from which to grow taller.

My rich dad helped me learn how to deal with deep emotional disappointments. Rich dad would often say, 'The reason there are few self-made rich people is because few people can tolerate disappointment. Instead of learning to face disappointment, they spend their lives avoiding it.'

He also said, 'Instead of avoiding it, be prepared for it. Disappointment is an important part of learning. Just as we learn from our mistakes, we gain character from our disappointments.'

Following are some of the words of advice he gave me over the years:

1. **Expect to be disappointed.** Rich dad often said, 'Only fools expect everything to go the way they want. To expect to be disappointed does not mean being passive or a defeated loser. Expecting to be disappointed is a way of mentally and emotionally preparing yourself to be ready for surprises that you may not want. By being emotionally prepared, you can act with calm and dignity when things do not go your way. If you're calm, you can think better.'

   Many times I have seen people with great new business ideas. Their excitement lasts for about a month, then the disappointments begin to wear them down. Soon, their excitement is diminished, and all you hear them say is, 'That was a good idea, but it didn't work.'

   It's not the idea that didn't work. It was disappointment that worked harder. They allowed their impatience to turn into disappointment and then they allowed the disappointment to defeat them. Many times this impatience is the result of them not receiving immediate financial reward. Business owners and investors may wait for years to see cash flow from a business or investment, but they go into it with the knowledge that success may take time. They also know that when success is achieved the financial reward will be well worth the wait.

2. **Have a mentor standing by.** In the front of your phone book are listings for the hospital, fire department and police department. I have the same list of numbers for financial emergencies, except they are the phone numbers of my mentors.

   Often, before I go into a deal or venture, I call one of

my friends and explain what I'm doing and what I intend to accomplish. I also ask them to stand by in case I find myself in over my head, which is often.

Recently, I was negotiating for a large piece of real estate. The seller was playing hardball and changing the terms at the closing. He knew I wanted the property, and he was doing his best to get more money from me at the last minute. Having a hot temper, my emotions went out of control. Instead of blowing the deal by yelling and shouting, which is my normal inclination, I simply asked if I could use the phone to call my partner.

After talking to three of my friends, who were standing by, and getting their advice on how to handle the situation, I calmed down and learned three new ways to negotiate I had not known before. The deal never went through, but I still use those three negotiation techniques today – techniques I would never have learned if I had not gone into the deal at all. That knowledge is priceless.

The point is, we can never know everything beforehand, and we often only learn things when we need to learn them. That is why I recommend you try new things and expect disappointment, but always have a mentor standing by to coach you through the experience. Many people never start projects simply because they do not have all the answers. You will never have all the answers, but begin anyway. As my friend Keith Cunningham always says, 'Many people will not head down the street until all the lights are green. That is why they don't go anywhere.'

3. **Be kind to yourself.** One of the most painful aspects about making a mistake and being disappointed or failing at something is not what other people say about us. It is how hard we are on ourselves. Most people who make mistakes often

beat themselves up far harder than anyone else would. They should turn themselves into the police for personal emotional abuse.

I have found that people who are hard on themselves mentally and emotionally are often too cautious when taking risks, or adopting new ideas, or attempting something new. It is hard to learn anything new if you punish yourself or blame someone else for your personal disappointments.

4. **Tell the truth.** One of the worst punishments I ever received as a child was the day I accidentally broke my sister's front tooth. She ran home to tell my dad, and I ran to hide. After my father found me, he was very angry.

He scolded me, 'The reason I am punishing you is not because you broke your sister's tooth . . . but because you ran away.'

Financially, there have been many times I could have run away from my mistakes. Running away is an easy thing to do but my dad's words have served me well for most of my life.

In short, we all make mistakes. We all feel upset and disappointed when things do not go our way. Yet, the difference lies in how we internally process that disappointment. Rich dad summarized it this way. He said, 'The size of your success is measured by the strength of your desire; the size of your dream; and how you handle disappointment along the way.'

In the next few years, we are going to have financial changes that will test our courage. It is the people who are most in control of their emotions, who do not let their emotions hold them back, and who have the emotional maturity to learn new financial skills who will flourish in the years ahead.

As Bob Dylan sang, 'The times they are a-changing.'

And the future belongs to those who can change with the times and use personal disappointments as building blocks for the future.

Take Action

1) Make mistakes. That is why I recommend you start with baby steps. Remember that losing is part of winning. 'E's' and 'S's' were trained that making mistakes was not acceptable. 'B's' and 'I's' know that making mistakes is how they learn.

2) Put a little money down. Start small. If you find an investment you want to invest in, put a little money down. It's amazing how quickly your intelligence grows when you have some money on the line. Don't bet the ranch, your mortgage payment, or your child's college education. Simply put a little money down . . . and then pay attention and learn.

3) The key to this take action step is to TAKE ACTION!

Reading, watching and listening are all crucial to your education. But you must also start 'DOING'. Make offers on small real estate deals that will generate positive cash flow, join a network marketing company and learn about it from the inside, invest in some stock after researching the company. Seek advice from your mentor, financial or tax advisor if you need it. But as Nike says, 'Just Do It!'

CHAPTER SEVENTEEN

Step 7: The Power Of Faith

What is your deepest fear?

In my senior year of high school, rich dad's son and I were lined up in front of a small group of students made up primarily of the leaders of the senior class. Our guidance counselor said to us, 'The two of you will never amount to anything.'

There was some snickering from some of the seniors as the guidance counselor continued. 'From now on, I am not going to waste any more time on either of you. I am only going to spend my time with these students who are the class leaders. You two are the class clowns with bad grades, and you will never amount to anything. Now get out of here.'

Biggest Favor Of All

That counselor did Mike and me the biggest favor of all. While what she said was true in many ways and her words hurt us deeply, her words also inspired both of us to strive even harder. Her words carried us through college and into our own businesses.

High School Reunion

A few years ago, Mike and I went back to our high school reunion, always an interesting experience. It was nice to visit with people with whom we had spent three years during a period of time when none of us really knew who we were. It was also interesting to see that most of the so-called senior leaders had not become successful in the years after high school.

I tell this story because Mike and I were not academic whiz kids. We were neither financial geniuses nor athletic stars. For the most part, we were slow-to-average learners and students. We were not leaders in our class. In my opinion, we were not as naturally gifted as our fathers. Yet it was our guidance counselor's stinging words and the snickering from our classmates that gave us the fire to plod along, to learn from our mistakes, and to keep going in both good times and bad times.

Just because you did not do well in school, were not popular, are not good in math, are rich or poor, or have other reasons to sell yourself short – none of it counts in the long run. Those so-called shortcomings only count if you think they count.

For those of you who are considering embarking on your own financial fast track, you may have some doubts about your abilities. All I can say is trust that you have everything you need right now to be successful financially. All it takes to bring out your natural God-given gifts is your desire, determination and a deep faith that you have a genius and a gift that is unique.

Look In The Mirror And Listen To The Words

A mirror reflects back more than just a visual image. A mirror often reflects back our thoughts. How often have we seen people, look in the mirror and say such things as:

'Oh, I look horrible.'

'Have I put on that much weight?'

'I'm really getting old.'

or

'My, my, my! I am damned good looking. I am God's gift to women.'

294

Thoughts Are Reflections

As I said, mirrors reflect back much more than just what the eyes see. Mirrors also reflect back our thoughts, often our opinions of ourselves. These thoughts or opinions are much more important than our outwardly appearance.

Many of us have met people who are beautiful on the outside, but inside they think they're ugly. Or people who are greatly loved by others, but they cannot love themselves. Our deepest thoughts are often reflections of our souls. Thoughts are a reflection of our love for ourselves, our egos, our dislike of ourselves, how we treat ourselves, and our overall opinion of ourselves.

Money Does Not Stay With People Who Do Not Trust Themselves

Personal truths are often spoken in moments of peak emotions.

After explaining the *CASHFLOW Quadrant* to a class or an individual I give them a moment to decide their next step. First they decide which quadrant they are in, which is easy because it's simply the quadrant that generates the most money for them. Second, I ask them, which quadrant they would like to move to, if they need to move.

They then look at the *Quadrant* and make their choices.

Some people look and say, 'I'm happy exactly where I am.'

Others say, 'I'm not happy with where I am, but I am not willing to change or move at this time.'

And then there are people who are unhappy where they are, and know they need to do something immediately. People in this condition often speak most clearly about their personal truths. They use words that reflect their opinions of themselves, words that reflect their souls. And that is why I say, 'Personal truths are spoken at moments of peak emotions.'

At these moments of truth I often hear:

'I can't do that. I can't move from "S" to "B". Are you crazy? I have a wife and three kids to feed.'

'I can't do that. I can't wait five years before I get another paycheck.'

'Invest? You want me to lose all my money don't you?'

'I don't have any money to invest.'

'I need more information before I do anything.'

'I tried that before. It will never work.'

'I don't need to know how to read financial statements. I can get by.'

'I don't have to worry. I'm still young.'

'I'm not smart enough.'

'I would do it if I could find the right people to do it with me.'

'My husband would never go for it.'

'My wife would never understand.'

'What would my friends say?'

'I would if I was younger.'

'It's too late for me.'

'It's not worth it.'

'I'm not worth it.'

All Words Are Mirrors

Personal truths are spoken at moments of peak emotion. All words are mirrors for they reflect back some insight as to what people think about themselves, even though they may be speaking about someone else.

My Best Advice

For those of you who are ready to move from one quadrant to another, the most important advice I know to give you is to be very aware of your words. Especially be aware of the words that come from your heart, your stomach, and your soul. If you are going to make a change, you must be aware of the thoughts and words generated by your emotions. If you cannot be aware of when your emotions are doing your thinking, you will never survive the journey. You will hold yourself back. For even if you are talking about somebody else, for example by saying, 'My spouse will never understand.' You are really saying something more about yourself. You may be using your spouse as an excuse for your own inaction, or you might actually be saying 'I don't have the courage or communication skills to convey these new ideas to her.' All words are mirrors that provide opportunities for you to look into your soul.

Or you might say,

'I can't stop working and start my own business. I have a mortgage and a family to think about.'

You might be saying:

'I'm tired. I don't want to do anything more.'

or,

'I really don't want to learn anything more.'

These are personal truths.

Personal Truths Are Also Personal Lies

These are truths and they are also lies. If you lie to yourself, I would say the journey will never be completed. So my best advice is to listen to your doubts, fears, and limiting thoughts, and then dig deeper for the deeper truth.

For example saying 'I'm tired, I don't want to learn something new' may be a truth but it is also a lie. The real truth may be 'If I don't learn something new, I'll be even more tired.' And even deeper than that, 'The truth is I love learning new things. I would love to learn new things and be excited about life again. Maybe whole new worlds would open to me.' Once you can get to that point of the deeper truth, you may find a part of you that is powerful enough to help you change.

Our Journey

For Kim and me to move forward we first had to be willing to live with the opinions and criticisms we individually had about ourselves. We had to be willing to live with the personal thoughts that kept us small, but not let them stop us. Occasionally the pressure would go to the boiling point and our self-criticisms would flare up and I would blame her for my self doubts and she would blame me for hers. Yet, we both knew before starting out on this journey that the only thing we had to face was ultimately our own personal doubts, criticisms and inadequacies. Our real job as husband and wife, business partners, and soul mates along this journey was to keep reminding each other that each of us was much more powerful than our individual doubts, pettiness, and inadequacies. In that process, we learned to trust ourselves more. The ultimate goal for us was more than to simply get rich; it was to learn to be trustworthy with ourselves as well as with money.

Remember the only person that determines the thoughts you choose to believe about yourself is you. So the reward from the journey is not only the freedom that money buys but the trust you gain in yourself . . . for they really are the same thing. My best advice to you is to prepare daily to be bigger than your smallness. In my opinion, the reason most people stop and turn back from their dreams is because the tiny person found inside each of us beats the person that is bigger.

Even though you may not be good at everything, take time developing what you need to learn and your world will change rapidly. Never run from what you know you need to learn. Face your fears and doubts, and new worlds will open to you.

Take Action
Believe in yourself and start today!

CHAPTER EIGHTEEN
In Summary

These are the seven steps my wife and I used to move from being homeless to being financially free in a few short years. These seven steps helped us find our own financial fast track and we continue to use them today. I trust they can assist you in charting your own course to financial freedom.

To do that, I recommend being true to yourself. If you are not yet a long-term investor, get yourself there as fast as you can. What does this mean? Sit down and map out a plan to get control of your spending habits. Minimize your debt and liabilities. Live within your means and then increase your means. Find out how much invested per month, for how many months, at a realistic rate of return it will take to reach your goals. Goals such as: At what age do you plan to stop working? How much money per month will you need to live at the standard you desire?

Simply having a long-term plan that reduces your consumer debt while putting away a small amount of money regularly will give you a head start if you start early enough and keep an eye on what you're doing.

At this level, keep it simple. Don't get fancy.

The reason I introduce you to the *CASHFLOW Quadrant,*

the 7 Levels of Investors and my three types of investors is to offer you many glimpses into who you are, what your interests may be, and who you want to ultimately become. I like to believe that anyone can find their own unique path to the financial fast track, regardless of which quadrant they operate from. Yet, it is ultimately up to you to find your own path.

Remember what I said in a previous chapter: 'Your boss's job is to give you a job. It's your job to make yourself rich.'

Are you ready to stop hauling water buckets and begin building pipelines of cash flow to support you, your family and your lifestyle?

Minding your own business might be difficult and sometimes confusing, especially at first. There is a lot to learn, regardless of how much you know. It is a lifelong process. But the good news is that the hardest part of the process is at the start. Once you make the commitment, life really does get easier and easier. Minding your business is not hard to do. It's just common sense.

The Quick Reference Guide to Wealth

by Alan Jacques*, Inspired by Robert Kiyosaki

	Broke Masses
1. Who	Employees
2. Education	High school or college graduate
3. Major financial goal	To survive until next payday
4. Focus	Salary or hourly wage
5. Cash Flow Management (CFM)	'How much do I have in my wallet?'
6. Definition of an asset	A 6-pack in the fridge
7. Home	Would like to own one
8. Investment vehicles	• Government pension • Lotteries
9. Investment sources	The government
10. Investment systems	• Hope
11. Expected rate of return	Get rich quick
12. Risk	Has no idea how to evaluate

Successful Middle Class Investor	Rich
Employees & self-employed	Business owners & investors
• Values education, often college graduate • Attends courses & seminars on investing	Values only 'street smart' education, often acquired from peers and/or self-learned
To build up a significant net worth by age 55–65	Freedom
Net worth	Cash flow
Understands the value of CFM	Understands that CFM is the foundation to all wealth
Anything that has market value	Anything that produces positive cash flow
One of their most important assets	A home is a liability, not an asset
• mutual funds • blue chip stocks • real estate: condos, houses & duplexes	• stocks: IPOs as investors and/ or key shareholders • real estate: larger projects • businesses
Invests in financial products created by others	Create products and services to sell to the Middle Class and the masses
• dollar cost averaging (DCA) • low down real estate systems	• Create their own and/or modify others • Often learn from other rich investors who are their peers
12% to 30%	50% to 500%+++
Accepts moderate risk	Most investments are low or very low risk

	Broke Masses
13. What Works	If it doesn't work, keep doing it.
14. Time horizon	Next payday
15. Real Estate	Would like some
16. Most valuable resource	Paycheck
17. Why work?	Work for the weekend
18. Advisors	Broke friends & family
19. Resources	• TV
20. Key indicator event	Savings account with $100 in it
21. Question & Answers	Don't really understand the distinction
22. Delegation	'If you want it done right, you have to do it yourself.'

Alan Jacques is president of a successful consulting company in Canada. He is a great teacher of money, wealth and entrepreneurial business.

Successful Middle Class Investor	Rich
Learn what works and keep doing it no matter what	Keep learning and innovate, innovate, innovate
Long term	Tailored to each goal and/ or investment
Buy & hold, waits for it to go up in value	'You make money when you buy, not when you sell.'
Investments	Time
Work for money of which 10–20% goes to investments	Money works so they don't have to
Financial planners, accountants	Themselves, each other, coaches, selected professionals
• *The Millionaire Next Door* • *The Wealthy Barber*	• *Rich Dad/Poor Dad* • *The CASHFLOW Quadrant* • *The CASHFLOW Game* • Robert Kiyosaki tape sets
$1 million in net worth	Passive income exceeds expenses
Asks questions and seeks the right answer	Knows there are many answers
'You can delegate what you don't know.'	'If you don't know the fundamentals, you can get slaughtered!'

*Recommended Reading

For Improving Your Financial Intelligence

At the Crest of the Tidal Wave, (Economics) *by Robert Prechter*

Awaken The Giant Within, (Personal Development) *by Anthony Robbins*

Creating Wealth, (Real Estate) *by Robert Allen*

Deals on Wheels, (Real Estate) *by Lonnie Scruggs*

E-Myth, (Business) *by Michael Gerber*

Emotional Intelligence, (Personal Development) *by Daniel Goleman*

God Wants You To Be Rich, (Wealth) *by Paul Zane Pilzer*

The Great Boom Ahead, (Economics) *by Harry S. Dent, Jr*

How To Make Money in Stocks, (Stocks) *by William J. O'Neil*

Influence, (Personal Development) *by Robert Cialdini*

Over The Top, (Sales) *by Zig Ziglar*

Rich Dad Poor Dad, (Personal Finance) *by Robert Kiyosaki with Sharon Lechter*

The Sovereign Individual, (Economics) *by James Dale Davidson and Lord William Rees-Mogg*

Stone Soup, (Leadership) *by Marcia Brown*

Trade Your Way To Financial Freedom, (Trading) *by Dr Van Tharp*

Trading For a Living, (Trading) *by Dr Alexander Elder*

The Wealth of Nations, (Economics) *by Adam Smith*

Think and Grow Rich, (Wealth) *by Napolean Hill*

Unlimited Wealth, (Wealth) *by Paul Zane Pilzer*

What Works On Wall Street, (Stocks) *by James O'Shaughnessy*

Who Stole the American Dream?, (Network Marketing) *by Burke Hedges*

The Worldly Philosophers, (Economics) *by Robert Heilbronner*

*Audio Tape Sets Recommended

Closing the Sale, (Sales) *by Raymond Aaron*
Goals, Crossing the Goal Line, (Goal Setting) *by Raymond Aaron*
Secrets of the Great Investors, (Investing) *by Knowledge Products*
Power-Talk, (Personal Development) *by Anthony Robbins*

*These books and tapes are suggested resources and may be time sensitive. We always recommend seeking your own professional, legal, financial and investment advice.

RICH DAD, POOR DAD

Robert T. Kiyosaki with Sharon L. Lechter C.P.A.

'The main reason people struggle financially is because they have spent years in school but learned nothing about money. The result is that people learn to work for money . . . but never learn to have money work for them.'
Robert T. Kiyosaki

Rich Dad, Poor Dad

WILL . . .

Explode the myth that you need to earn a high income to become rich.

Challenge the belief that your house is an asset.

Show parents why they can't rely on the school system to teach their kids about money.

Define once and for all an asset and a liability.

Teach you what to teach your kids about money for their future financial success.

RICH DAD'S
RICH KID, SMART KID

Robert T. Kiyosaki with
Sharon L. Lechter C.P.A.

Rich Kid, Smart Kid is written for parents who value
education, who want to give their child a financial and
academic head start in life, and are willing to take an
active role to make that happen.

In the Information Age a good education is more
important than ever. But the current education system may
not be providing all the information your child needs. This
book fills in the gaps: to help give your child the same
inspiring and practical financial knowledge that Robert
Kiyosaki's rich dad gave him. Rich Kid, Smart Kid will
show you how to awaken your child's love of learning
using the same methods that Robert's smart dad used to
help Robert stay in school, even though he had bad grades
and often wanted to drop out.

'Rich Kid, Smart Kid provides an insight into how
your children think and learn best. Armed with this
knowledge you can help your children achieve their
full potential in life.'
Sharon Lechter

Time Warner Paperback titles available by post:

☐	Rich Dad, Poor Dad	Robert T. Kiyosaki	£7.99
☐	Rich Kid, Smart Kid	Robert T. Kiyosaki	£12.99
☐	Rich Dad's Retire Young, Retire Rich	Robert T. Kiyosaki	£7.99
☐	Rich Dad, Poor Dad (audio tape)	Robert T. Kiyosaki	£17.99
☐	Rich Dad, Poor Dad (CD)	Robert T. Kiyosaki	£18.99
☐	Rich Dad's Cashflow Quadrant (CD)	Robert T. Kiyosaki	£14.99
☐	Rich Dad's Classics (audio tape)	Robert T. Kiyosaki	£35.00
☐	Rich Dad's Guide to Investing (audio tape)	Robert T. Kiyosaki	£17.99
☐	Rich Dad's Guide to Investing (CD)	Robert T. Kiyosaki	£18.99
☐	Rich Dad's Rich Kid, Smart Kid (audio tape)	Robert T. Kiyosaki	£17.99
☐	Rich Dad's Rich Kid, Smart Kid (CD)	Robert T. Kiyosaki	£18.99

The prices shown above are correct at time of going to press. However, the publishers reserve the right to increase prices on covers from those previously advertised without prior notice.

timewarner
paperbacks

TIME WARNER PAPERBACKS
P.O. Box 121, Kettering, Northants NN14 4ZQ
Tel: 01832 737525, Fax: 01832 733076
Email: aspenhouse@FSBDial.co.uk

POST AND PACKING:
Payments can be made as follows: cheque, postal order (payable to Time Warner Paperbacks) or by credit cards. Do not send cash or currency.

All U.K. Orders   **FREE OF CHARGE**
E.E.C. & Overseas   25% of order value

Name (Block Letters) _____

Address _____

_____

Post/zip code: _____

☐ Please keep me in touch with future Time Warner publications

☐ I enclose my remittance £_____

☐ I wish to pay by Visa/Access/Mastercard/Eurocard

Card Expiry Date

_____